Mindfulness in Golf

Copyright Notice:

© 2024 Nigel Lefley – All rights reserved.

No part of this book may be reproduced, stored in a retrieval system, or transmitted in any form or by any means, electronic, mechanical, photocopying, recording, or otherwise, without the prior written permission of the author or the publisher.

Legal Notices:

This book is protected by copyright law. It is intended solely for personal use. You may not amend, distribute, sell, use, quote, or paraphrase any part of this book without the prior written consent of the author or publisher.

Disclaimer:

The information contained in this book is for educational and entertainment purposes only. All efforts have been made to present accurate, up-to-date, and reliable information; however, no warranties of any kind are expressed or implied. The reader understands that the author is not rendering legal, financial, medical, or professional advice. Sources of information have been cited where applicable.

By reading this book, the reader agrees not to hold the author or publisher liable for any losses, whether direct or indirect, resulting from the use of the information contained within this book. This includes, but is not limited to, any errors, omissions, or inaccuracies.

Table of Contents

About the Author 4

Chapter 1. Introduction to Mindfulness 5

1.1: Definition and Principles of Mindfulness 6

1.2 Benefits of Mindfulness in Sports and Daily Life 9

Chapter 2: The Connection Between Mindfulness and Golf 17

2.1: How Mindfulness Can Improve Focus and Reduce Stress on the Golf Course 18

2.2: Success Stories of Professional Golfers Who Use Mindfulness 25

Chapter 3: Mindful Practices for Golfers 34

3.1: Breathing Techniques to Maintain Calmness and Focus 34

3.2: Visualisation Exercises to Improve Performance 48

3.3: Meditation Practices for Mental Clarity and Stress Reduction 52

Chapter 4: Pre-Game Mindfulness Routine 64

4.1: Warm-Up Exercises That Incorporate Mindfulness 64

4.2: Setting Intentions and Mental Preparation Before Playing 73

Chapter 5: Mindful Strategies During Play 83

5.1: Staying Present: Techniques to Focus on the Current Shot 83

5.2: Handling Pressure and High-Stress Situations Mindfully 89

Chapter 6: Post-Game Reflection 99

6.1: Techniques for Reflecting on Your Game Without Judgment 99

6.2: Learning from Mistakes and Celebrating Successes Mindfully 111

Chapter 7: Mindfulness Off the Course 121

7.1: Incorporating Mindfulness into Daily Life for Overall Well-Being 121

7.2: Building a Lifestyle That Supports Mental and Physical Health 131

Chapter 8: Tools and Resources 142

8.1: Recommended Apps, Books, and Resources for Further Mindfulness Training 142

8.2: Interviews and Stories from Golfers Who Practice Mindfulness 154

About the Author

Golf has always held a special place in my life, both as a sport and as a personal journey. But it wasn't until I discovered mindfulness that I truly began to understand the mental side of the game and how it directly influenced my performance. Like many amateur golfers, I spent countless hours working on my swing, analysing my mechanics, and practicing shots. Yet, I often found myself frustrated or anxious, especially during moments when it felt like my game was slipping away.

My introduction to mindfulness came at a time when I was looking for a way to calm my mind, not just on the course but in my day-to-day life. Mindfulness practices showed me the power of presence—of focusing my attention on the here and now. It was a revelation to realise how much of my frustration and inconsistency stemmed from distractions or the pressures I placed on myself. Through mindfulness, I began to tune into my emotions, my body, and my intentions with greater clarity.

Applying mindfulness to my golf game transformed the experience. Instead of getting bogged down by a bad shot or worrying about future holes, I started using mindfulness techniques to centre myself on every shot, regardless of its outcome. I developed a pre-shot routine that grounded me in the present, releasing both anxiety and expectations. I focused on how my body felt, noticed my breathing, and let go of judgments about my performance.

The benefits have been profound. Not only has my game improved, but my enjoyment of the game has deepened. I find that I recover from mistakes more easily, stay composed under pressure, and experience a steadier, more fulfilling rhythm while playing. Mindfulness has allowed me to connect with golf on a more meaningful level, transforming it from a game of results to a practice of presence and personal growth.

This book is my attempt to share that journey with you and to offer tools that can bring greater peace, focus, and fulfilment to your game. Whether you're a seasoned player or a casual weekend golfer, I believe mindfulness has the power to enhance not only your performance but also your connection to the game in ways you may never have imagined.

Chapter 1. Introduction to Mindfulness

In a world that often feels rushed and chaotic, the practice of mindfulness stands as a beacon of clarity and calm. Defined as the quality of being present and fully engaged with the current moment, mindfulness invites us to step away from the distractions of the past and future, allowing us to appreciate the richness of each experience as it unfolds. This book is your gateway to understanding and integrating mindfulness into your life, particularly within the context of golf—a sport that marries physical skill with profound mental acuity.

Mindfulness is more than just a trend; it is a practice rooted in ancient traditions that has been adopted around the globe for its powerful benefits. From reducing stress and enhancing emotional resilience to improving focus and performance, mindfulness offers a transformative approach to navigating life's challenges, both on and off the golf course. As athletes and individuals striving for personal growth, we often find ourselves caught in cycles of self-doubt, anxiety, and distraction. Mindfulness provides the tools to break these cycles, allowing us to cultivate a healthier relationship with ourselves and our surroundings.

In this book, we will explore the fundamental principles of mindfulness, delving into practical techniques and exercises that can enrich your golfing experience and overall well-being. You will discover how mindfulness can improve concentration and performance, reduce the pressure associated with competition, and enhance your connection to the game. Each chapter is designed to guide you through various aspects of mindfulness—it's not merely a mental exercise, but a holistic approach that encompasses body, spirit, and breath.

As we embark on this journey together, you will encounter stories of fellow golfers who have embraced mindfulness and experienced profound transformations in their games and lives. Their experiences will serve as powerful reminders of the positive impact that being present can have, not only on the golf course but in every facet of life.

Mindfulness is a practice that requires patience, commitment, and openness; it is a path rather than a destination. Throughout this book, you will find practical techniques, exercises, and reflections to help cultivate mindfulness as an integral part of your daily life. My hope is that by embracing these practices, you will learn to appreciate the journey of golf and life with greater awareness, love, and joy.

Welcome to the exploration of mindfulness—a journey toward clarity, focus, and a deeper connection to yourself and the game you love. Together, let's unlock the transformative power of being truly present, one shot at a time

1.1: Definition and Principles of Mindfulness

Mindfulness is a term that has gained considerable attention in recent years, transcending its origins to become a widely recognised practice embraced by individuals across various walks of life. At its core, mindfulness refers to the practice of being fully present in the moment, engaging with one's thoughts, feelings, and surroundings without judgment. This chapter delves into the definition of mindfulness, its foundational principles, and its relevance not only in daily living but also in enhancing performance in the game of golf.

Understanding Mindfulness

To define mindfulness, we can turn to Jon Kabat-Zinn, a pioneer in bringing the concept of mindfulness to the Western world. He articulately describes mindfulness as "the awareness that arises from paying attention, on purpose, in the present moment, and nonjudgmentally." This concise yet powerful definition encapsulates the essence of mindfulness, highlighting its core components: intentionality, presence, and acceptance.

Mindfulness invites individuals to engage deeply with the here and now, cultivating an acute awareness of their thoughts, feelings, and surroundings without the clutter of judgment or distraction. By focusing on the present moment, practitioners are encouraged to observe their experiences as they are, rather than through the lens of expectation or regret. This approach creates a safe space for self-discovery and understanding, where one can learn to navigate life's complexities with greater clarity and composure.

The practice of mindfulness is simple in its principles yet profound in its implications. It empowers individuals to cultivate a state of awareness that enhances their ability to respond to life's challenges thoughtfully and intentionally. By embracing mindfulness, we can break free from the chaos of an overly busy mind, allowing ourselves to experience life with a renewed sense of curiosity and openness. As we explore the intricacies of mindfulness throughout this book, it is important to remember that this practice serves as a pathway not only to improved focus and performance but also to a richer, more engaged experience of life itself.

The Four Foundations of Mindfulness

Mindfulness is anchored in four foundational principles that collectively enhance its efficacy in promoting a balanced mental state. These pillars serve as the framework through which individuals can cultivate greater awareness, emotional resilience, and presence in both their golfing pursuits and everyday lives.

1. **Attention:** At its core, mindfulness encourages individuals to develop focused attention on their thoughts, feelings, and sensations. This process involves observing experiences as they arise without becoming overwhelmed or distracted. Whether you find yourself on the golf course preparing to take a swing or navigating the daily challenges of life, honing your attention is essential. Cultivating this focused awareness allows you to engage deeply with the present moment, facilitating a clearer understanding of your internal landscape and enhancing your responses to the world around you.
2. **Non-Judgment:** Central to the practice of mindfulness is the principle of non-judgment. This involves approaching your thoughts and feelings with curiosity and openness rather than labelling them as 'good' or 'bad.' By embracing a non-judgmental stance, mindfulness fosters an environment of self-compassion, allowing golfers to learn from each experience without dwelling on perceived failures. This acceptance creates a safe space in which individuals can explore their emotions and thoughts freely, ultimately leading to a deeper understanding of themselves and their game.
3. **Present Moment Awareness:** Mindfulness emphasises the importance of fully engaging with the present moment, encouraging individuals to avoid the common pitfalls of dwelling on the past or worrying about the future. This principle is particularly crucial in golf, where mental distractions can derail performance. By centering our awareness in the here and now, we empower ourselves to play our best game, focusing on each swing and shot as a unique opportunity. Present moment awareness not only enhances our performance on the course but also enriches our everyday experiences, inviting us to savour the richness of life.
4. **Self-Regulation:** Through the practice of mindfulness, individuals cultivate the ability to recognise and manage their emotional responses effectively. This self-regulation enhances emotional intelligence, allowing golfers to maintain composure in high-pressure situations. Whether facing a challenging putt with the game on the line or managing internal stressors during a round, the skills developed through mindfulness enable individuals to focus on strategy and execution. By learning to navigate their emotions with clarity, golfers

can approach each situation thoughtfully, improving their overall performance and enjoyment of the game.

Together, these four foundational principles of mindfulness create a robust framework for personal growth, enhanced performance, and deeper engagement with the world. By embracing attention, non-judgment, present moment awareness, and self-regulation, individuals can cultivate a mindful approach to both golf and life, leading to transformative outcomes that resonate far beyond the course. As you explore these principles further in this book, consider how they can be integrated into your daily life and practice, unlocking the full potential of mindfulness and enriching your overall experience.

Benefits of Mindfulness

The practice of mindfulness extends far beyond the realm of mental clarity; it encompasses a broad spectrum of psychological and emotional benefits that can significantly enhance a golfer's experience, both on and off the course. Extensive research has demonstrated that engaging in mindfulness practices can lead to notable reductions in anxiety, improved focus, and enhanced emotional regulation. For golfers, these advantages are particularly impactful, as they translate directly into heightened performance while playing.

As golfers immerse themselves in mindfulness, they develop greater resilience to stressors that can derail concentration and disrupt their game. The ability to remain composed under pressure enables players to better navigate the ups and downs of competition, maintaining a clear mind that fosters effective decision-making and execution of skills. This mental fortitude is crucial for coping with both the external pressures of the game and the internal dialogue that often accompanies competitive play.

Moreover, the benefits of mindfulness extend to overall well-being, promoting a profound sense of peace and contentment in daily life. As individuals cultivate mindfulness, they learn to appreciate the richness of each moment—whether on the golf course or in everyday experiences. This heightened awareness fosters a deeper connection to the game itself, allowing golfers to find joy in the process rather than solely focusing on the outcomes.

In embracing mindfulness, golfers transform their engagement with the sport, creating a more fulfilling and enriching experience. This practice nurtures not only a healthier mind-set but also a more profound relationship with oneself and the environment. As mindfulness takes root, players can unlock the transformative potential of each round, experiencing golf as a journey of growth, connection, and self-discovery.

Mindfulness in Golf

Incorporating mindfulness into one's golf practice can truly be a game changer. Golf is a uniquely demanding sport, continually presenting a myriad of distractions—from the external pressures of competition to the internal expectations and self-imposed standards we carry. These distractions can easily derail focus and diminish enjoyment. However, by embracing mindfulness, golfers have the opportunity to transform their approach to the game, discovering joy and clarity in every shot they take.

This chapter lays the groundwork for understanding the profound impact mindfulness can have on your golfing experience. Here, we will explore the key principles of mindfulness and how they can be effectively integrated into the various aspects of the game. The subsequent chapters will delve into practical techniques and exercises specifically designed to enhance mindfulness on the course. These strategies will empower you to navigate challenges with greater resilience while cultivating a more fulfilling and focused approach to your rounds.

As we embark on this exploration together, it's important to remember that mindfulness is not merely a goal to achieve but a continuous practice—a dynamic journey of learning, growing, and being present in each moment. Mindfulness invites you to engage deeply with the art of golf, enabling you to appreciate the beauty of the game while honing your skills. By committing to this journey of mindfulness, you will uncover the potential to enhance not only your performance but also your overall enjoyment of the sport. Let us begin this transformative experience, cultivating a mindful practice that will enrich your time on the course and in life.

1.2 Benefits of Mindfulness in Sports and Daily Life

In today's fast-paced, distraction-laden world, the significance of mindfulness has never been more pronounced. As we navigate the complexities of modern life—rushing from one responsibility to another, consumed by digital notifications, and burdened by chronic stress—the practice of mindfulness emerges as a crucial antidote. Athletes and everyday individuals alike are increasingly recognising how this ancient practice can enhance not only performance in sports but also the overall quality of life.

This chapter delves into the myriad benefits of mindfulness, illuminating its transformative power in both athletic contexts and daily living. Through the cultivation of awareness and presence, individuals can experience profound changes that enhance mental clarity, emotional resilience, and physical well-being. Research has shown that mindfulness contributes to reduced stress and anxiety, improved focus and concentration, and better emotional regulation—benefits that are invaluable both on the field and in everyday interactions.

We will explore how athletes integrate mindfulness into their training regimens, learning to remain present under the pressures of competition, and how this practice translates to improved performance on their respective fields or courts. Additionally, we will examine how individuals in everyday life can apply mindfulness to enhance their relationships, decision-making, and overall sense of fulfilment.

The journey toward a more mindful existence involves recognising the interconnectedness of our thoughts, emotions, and actions, and how they influence the quality of our lives. By embracing mindfulness, you can unlock the potential for positive change, leading to clearer thinking, greater satisfaction, and a more harmonious balance between mind and body.

As we embark on this exploration of the benefits of mindfulness, you will gain insights into how cultivating this practice can lead to lasting transformations, enriching both your athletic pursuits and your daily experiences. Prepare to discover how the simple act of being present can create profound shifts in your life, fostering resilience and joy in all that you do.

Enhanced Focus and Concentration

One of the most immediate and impactful benefits of mindfulness is its remarkable ability to sharpen focus and concentration. In the realm of sports, the capacity to maintain unwavering attention on the task at hand is paramount. For golfers, this means remaining fully present during each swing, effectively blocking out distractions from the crowd and the pressures that accompany competition. Mindfulness practices equip athletes with the tools to direct their attention intentionally, fostering a mental space conducive to peak performance.

Research indicates that athletes who actively engage in mindfulness report significant improvements in both concentration and mental clarity. By training themselves to be more aware of their thoughts and feelings, these athletes develop the ability to enter a state of flow—a mental state characterised by complete immersion and focus in the activity. In this heightened state of awareness, golfers can respond to challenges with greater agility and creativity, navigating the complexities of each shot with clarity and poise.

Moreover, mindfulness enhances the golfer's ability to manage distractions, whether they originate from external sources, such as the noise of spectators, or internal pressures, such as self-doubt and anxiety. By cultivating a mindful mind-set, golfers learn to acknowledge distractions without judgment and gently redirect their focus to the task at hand. This shift allows them to maintain composure, enabling more consistent execution and ultimately translating to improved performance.

The mastery of focus and concentration achieved through mindfulness not only elevates game performance but also enriches the overall experience of playing golf. By embracing the present moment, golfers can find joy in the process, appreciating each swing and shot as a distinct opportunity for growth. In cultivating this enhanced mental acuity, mindfulness empowers athletes to excel not only in their sport but also in life, fostering a resilient and clear-minded approach to every challenge they face.

Reduced Anxiety and Stress

The psychological pressures faced by athletes can be immense, frequently leading to anxiety that hampers performance and detracts from the enjoyment of the game. In the high-stakes world of sports, the weight of expectations—from coaches, peers, and oneself—can become overwhelming. Fortunately, mindfulness practices provide individuals with essential tools to manage these pressures effectively and cultivate a more balanced state of mind.

By promoting heightened awareness of thoughts and emotions, mindfulness encourages a non-judgmental acceptance of anxiety. Rather than attempting to suppress or fight against these feelings, athletes learn to observe them with curiosity and openness. This shift allows them to recognise anxiety as a natural part of the competitive experience, effectively diminishing its power and influence over their performance. Observing anxiety without judgment transforms these feelings into manageable sensations, making it easier to maintain focus and composure during pivotal moments on the course.

Beyond the realm of sports, the benefits of reduced anxiety extend into everyday life, enhancing overall well-being. Mindfulness fosters emotional resilience, enabling individuals to navigate stressful situations with grace and poise. The ability to respond to challenges thoughtfully—rather than react impulsively—creates a more harmonious balance in life.

Incorporating mindful practices such as breathing exercises and meditation into daily routines can significantly contribute to this sense of calm. Deep, intentional breathing techniques help ground individuals in moments of tension, allowing them to return to a centred state. Similarly, regular meditation cultivates a practice of self-awareness that can transform how one engages with stressors in their environment.

The ripple effect of mindfulness in everyday life is substantial. As individuals learn to address anxiety and stress in healthy ways, they cultivate a greater sense of well-being that permeates all aspects of their lives. This newfound emotional resilience empowers golfers and non-golfers alike to approach both challenges and triumphs with clarity and confidence. By embracing mindfulness, you build the foundations for a more peaceful existence, where anxiety no longer holds sway over your experiences.

Improved Emotional Regulation

Mindfulness serves as a powerful teacher, guiding individuals toward heightened awareness of their emotions as they arise. This awareness is crucial for facilitating better emotional regulation, especially in high-pressure situations. For athletes, the golf course is often a stage for intense emotional experiences—be it the disappointment of a missed shot, the frustration of an erratic performance, or the exhilaration of a well-executed swing. By practicing mindfulness, athletes learn to acknowledge these emotions without allowing them to dictate their actions or cloud their judgment.

The ability to pause and observe one's emotional responses cultivates a greater sense of control and composure. Instead of being swept away by feelings like anger or anxiety, athletes can step back, recognise these emotions, and choose their responses thoughtfully. This practice not only enhances performance on the course but also transforms how athletes navigate the emotionally charged environment of competitive golf.

Moreover, the benefits of improved emotional regulation extend beyond sports; they significantly enhance daily life and interpersonal relationships.

As individuals cultivate mindfulness, they become more attuned to their emotional states, enabling them to respond to various situations with greater clarity and intention. This newfound awareness fosters healthier relationships and more effective communication, as individuals learn to engage with others thoughtfully rather than react impulsively.

In essence, mindfulness equips individuals with the tools to respond to emotional triggers with calmness and reason. Instead of allowing stress or frustration to dictate behaviour, they develop the capacity to engage in meaningful interactions, express themselves clearly, and navigate conflicts more harmoniously. By fostering emotional regulation through mindfulness, golfers and non-golfers alike can create a more fulfilling and connected life, enriched by the ability to handle life's challenges with grace and resilience.

Increased Resilience and Adaptability

Mindfulness is a transformative practice that fosters resilience—the capacity to bounce back from setbacks and overcome challenges with renewed strength. In the world of sports, particularly in golf, resilience is essential for navigating the inevitable ups and downs of competition. Mindful athletes develop a mind-set that redefines their relationship with failure, perceiving it not as an insurmountable barrier but as a valuable opportunity for growth. This shift in perspective encourages a greater willingness to embrace challenges, take risks, and learn from each experience on the course.

By practicing mindfulness, golfers learn to approach each round with a sense of curiosity and openness, acknowledging that mistakes are an intrinsic part of the game. Rather than succumbing to discouragement or frustration after a missed shot, they cultivate the ability to analyse the situation, glean lessons, and move forward with confidence. This resilient mind-set not only enhances performance but also enriches the overall experience of playing golf, transforming it into a journey of continuous learning and self-improvement.

The benefits of resilience cultivated through mindfulness extend well beyond the fairway. In daily life, mindfulness equips individuals to face adversity with a composed demeanour. Whether dealing with personal challenges, work-related stress, or unexpected changes, those who practice mindfulness are better able to adapt to shifting circumstances and navigate life's inevitable highs and lows with grace.

As individuals embrace mindfulness, they cultivate a deeper connection to their internal resources—their thoughts, emotions, and reactions—thus building a robust toolkit for handling difficulties. This enhanced resilience enables them to maintain perspective in challenging situations and encourages a proactive approach to problem-solving. By allowing mindfulness to inform their responses to adversity, individuals foster a greater sense of balance and well-being, making it easier to thrive in all facets of life.

In essence, mindfulness not only promotes resilience in the face of setbacks but also enhances adaptability in an ever-changing world. By embedding this practice into their lives, golfers and individuals alike unlock their potential to grow stronger through challenges, cultivating a sense of confidence that serves them well on and off the course.

Enhanced Physical Health

The advantages of mindfulness extend far beyond the mental and emotional realms; they significantly contribute to improved physical health as well. Research has consistently shown that mindfulness practices can lead to a variety of physiological benefits, including lowered blood pressure, reduced chronic pain, and enhanced overall well-being. For athletes, these benefits translate into tangible improvements in performance, as mindfulness fosters better recovery strategies and promotes injury prevention.

When golfers practice mindfulness, they cultivate an acute awareness of their bodies and the signals they convey. By learning to listen to physical cues—such as fatigue, tension, or strain—athletes can respond proactively to avoid injury and enhance their training regimens. This deeper connection with their physical state helps golfers optimise their performance by ensuring that they are in peak condition when it matters most.

In everyday life, the integration of mindfulness encourages healthier lifestyle choices that holistically support physical well-being. Mindful individuals are more likely to engage in regular exercise, practice balanced nutrition, and prioritise self-care activities. The heightened awareness brought about by mindfulness fosters a greater understanding of the mind-body connection, allowing individuals to make more informed and intentional decisions about their health.

For instance, mindfulness may lead to increased awareness of cravings and the emotional triggers behind them, promoting healthier eating habits and reducing the tendency to overindulge. Additionally, cultivating mindfulness can motivate individuals to embrace physical activities that bring them joy, rather than viewing exercise as a chore.

Ultimately, by recognising the intricate links between mind and body, individuals can adopt a holistic approach to health and well-being. This comprehensive perspective facilitates sustained physical vitality and resilience, ensuring golfers and everyday individuals alike can thrive in both their sporting endeavours and daily pursuits. In embracing mindfulness, you empower yourself not only to improve your physical health but also to foster a balanced, vibrant lifestyle that nourishes every aspect of your life.

Greater Enjoyment and Connection

One of the most profound benefits of mindfulness is its remarkable ability to enhance enjoyment and foster a deeper sense of satisfaction derived from our experiences. In the realm of sports, mindfulness allows athletes to immerse themselves fully in the game, savouring each moment, every swing, and the invaluable interactions with teammates. This heightened level of engagement creates a fulfilling experience that transcends mere outcomes, such as win-loss records.

When golfers practice mindfulness on the course, they become attuned to the intricacies of the game—the feel of the club in their hands, the sound of the ball striking the clubface, and the rhythm of their movements. This immersive quality brings an enriched sense of joy and fulfilment, transforming each round into a celebration of the sport itself. Athletes learn to appreciate the nuances of their practice, celebrating small achievements and personal growth along the way rather than solely fixating on competitive results.

Beyond the golf course, mindfulness extends its benefits to daily life by cultivating a deeper connection to oneself and to others. It encourages individuals to slow down and appreciate the small joys that can easily be overlooked in the hustle and bustle of everyday existence. A warm cup of coffee, the beauty of nature during a morning walk, or a moment shared with a friend—these seemingly ordinary experiences become opportunities for gratitude and connection.

By being present in everyday moments, individuals can enrich their experiences, leading to a more vibrant and meaningful life. Mindfulness empowers us to engage with the world more fully, allowing us to connect with our thoughts, emotions, and the people around us. This sense of connection not only enhances personal well-being but also strengthens relationships, as mindfulness fosters empathy, active listening, and deeper understanding.

The transformative power of mindfulness lies in its ability to shape our perceptions and deepen our experiences, both in sports and daily living. As you embrace mindfulness, you open yourself to a world of greater enjoyment, connection, and a profound appreciation for life's fleeting moments. Ultimately, the practice of mindfulness invites you to live not just reactively, but with intention and awareness, enriching your journey and fostering fulfilment in every aspect of your life.

Conclusion

The benefits of mindfulness in sports and daily life are profound and far-reaching. By enhancing focus, reducing anxiety, improving emotional regulation, fostering resilience, promoting physical health, and increasing enjoyment, mindfulness can transform the way individuals approach challenges both on the golf course and beyond.

As we continue this exploration of mindfulness in the context of golf, we will examine practical techniques to help incorporate these principles into your game, ensuring that you not only perform better but also find greater joy in the sport itself. Remember, each moment presents an opportunity for mindfulness—a chance to embrace the now, both in sports and in life.

Chapter 2: The Connection Between Mindfulness and Golf

Golf, often referred to as a game of precision and strategy, is uniquely positioned at the intersection of physical skill and mental acuity. While players hone their swings, putts, and course management, the true essence of the game often lies within the mind. The connection between mindfulness and golf is profound, offering athletes the opportunity to enhance their performance while fostering a deeper appreciation for the game itself.

As golfers, we frequently find ourselves faced with a multitude of distractions—ranging from the pressure of competition, the thoughts of previous shots, or even the expectations we place on ourselves. Mindfulness emerges as a powerful ally in navigating these challenges, supplying us with techniques to cultivate presence, focus, and resilience. It teaches us the importance of being fully engaged in each shot, cultivating awareness of our thoughts, emotions, and physical sensations.

In this chapter, we will explore how mindfulness impacts various aspects of the golfing experience. By understanding the mental state required to excel in golf, we can begin to recognise the vital role mindfulness plays in enhancing our performance. We will examine how being present in the moment not only improves focus but also nurtures emotional regulation, allowing golfers to respond to pressure more effectively.

We will also delve into the scientific underpinnings of mindfulness and its psychological benefits, illustrating how a mindful approach can transform not just our game, but our relationship with the sport. As we pave the way toward deeper understanding, we will highlight the stories of golfers who have embraced mindfulness, discovering the transformative effect it has had on their performance and personal growth.

By the end of this chapter, you will have gained insights into the rich connection between mindfulness and golf, setting the stage for the practices and techniques that will follow in subsequent chapters. As we embark on this exploration, we invite you to open your mind to the possibility that mindfulness can enhance not only your skill set but also your enjoyment of the game, allowing you to experience the beauty of golf in a whole new light. Welcome to a journey where every shot becomes an opportunity for growth, awareness, and connection.

2.1: How Mindfulness Can Improve Focus and Reduce Stress on the Golf Course

For many golfers, the course represents more than just a field of play; it is a sanctuary—an expansive canvas where skill meets serenity. Amid the natural beauty of rolling greens and majestic trees lies the potential for profound connection with the game. However, the golf course can also become a battleground where mental distractions and pressures threaten to derail even the most seasoned players. In these moments, the practice of mindfulness emerges as a powerful tool for enhancing focus and alleviating stress, offering golfers the mental clarity necessary to perform at their best.

Mindfulness equips players with the ability to anchor themselves in the present moment, providing an antidote to the noise of external distractions and internal anxieties. The pressures of competition, the weight of expectations, and the echoes of past mistakes can clutter the mind, leading to uncertainty and decreased performance. By cultivating mindfulness, golfers learn to navigate these challenges, honing their concentration and amplifying their capacity to engage with each shot fully.

In this chapter, we will explore how mindfulness practices can profoundly transform one's experience on the course. We will discuss specific techniques that promote heightened focus, such as mindful breathing, visualisation, and non-judgmental awareness, allowing golfers to maintain composure and clarity during play. By integrating these practices into their routines, players can develop a mind-set that views challenges as opportunities for growth rather than obstacles to success.

Additionally, the benefits of mindfulness extend beyond mere performance enhancement; they also contribute to a deeper enjoyment of the game. By fostering presence and appreciation for the moment, mindfulness allows golfers to immerse themselves in each swing, every putt, and the very essence of the game itself.

As we delve into the practices that cultivate mindfulness on the golf course, remember that the journey of mindfulness is an ongoing process—one marked by continuous learning and discovery. This chapter serves as a guide to help you unlock the transformative power of mindfulness, allowing you to improve focus, reduce stress, and truly enjoy the game of golf like never before. Embrace this opportunity to enhance your performance and deepen your connection to both the sport and yourself.

The Mental Landscape of Golf

Golf is as much a mental game as it is a physical one, demanding a unique blend of skill, strategy, and psychological fortitude. As players step onto the course, they are confronted with a myriad of challenges that test both their physical prowess and mental acuity. From evaluating distances and adjusting for wind conditions to managing their own expectations, golfers must navigate a complex mental landscape where clarity and focus are paramount.

However, the mental terrain can often become cluttered with intrusive thoughts—reminders of past mistakes, anxieties about upcoming shots, and the weight of external pressures. This mental noise can lead to inconsistent performance, as golfers struggle to concentrate amidst the chaos of their minds. The ability to maintain focus is frequently compromised when distractions cloud judgment, resulting in frustration and missed opportunities.

By integrating mindfulness into their practice, golfers can cultivate a clearer mental space that fosters enhanced performance. Mindfulness encourages players to centre their attention on the present moment, fully engaging with the shot at hand rather than becoming lost in a tangled web of worries and distractions. This intentional focus not only diminishes the power of negative thoughts but also enriches the golfing experience, allowing athletes to immerse themselves in the rhythm and flow of the game.

Furthermore, mindfulness offers golfers the tools to develop greater self-awareness—recognising when thoughts are drifting and gently redirecting their focus back to the task at hand. With increased emotional regulation, players can respond to challenges thoughtfully, embracing each shot as a new opportunity rather than a burden of expectation.

In essence, the mental landscape of golf is both a challenge and an opportunity. By fostering mindfulness, golfers can navigate this landscape with heightened clarity, allowing for more intentional play and an enriched connection to the game. As we delve deeper into the practices that promote mindfulness in golf, we will explore how to harness this powerful tool to transform your mental approach, improve consistency, and ultimately enhance your enjoyment of the sport.

Cultivating Present Moment Awareness

At the heart of mindfulness lies the essential practice of cultivating present moment awareness. For golfers, this means engaging fully with each shot, embracing the entirety of the experience from the tee to the green. By practicing mindfulness, players can learn to anchor themselves in the here and now—focusing their attention on key aspects such as their breathing, posture, and stance. This intentional focus serves to eliminate distractions, empowering golfers to concentrate solely on executing their swings with clarity and precision.

The ability to remain present transforms the way golfers approach their game. Instead of being side-tracked by past mistakes or apprehensive thoughts about future outcomes, they tap into the power of the moment, where performance is optimised. Developing present moment awareness allows players to feel the flow of their bodies as they swing, to sense the connection between their feet and the ground, and to be attuned to the subtle cues from the environment around them.

Incorporating techniques such as deep breathing or grounding exercises into a pre-shot routine creates a structured approach to fostering this mindfulness. For example, a golfer might pause before taking their shot to take a few deep, deliberate breaths, inhaling slowly through the nose and exhaling fully through the mouth. As they do this, they can focus on feeling their feet firmly planted on the ground, ensuring a stable foundation. By bringing awareness to their physical sensations, golfers can settle their minds, dispelling tension and anxiety.

This practice of deep breathing not only calms the nervous system but also enhances concentration, creating a mental environment conducive to peak performance. Grounding exercises, where players consciously connect with the earth beneath them, further reinforce this sense of stability and presence.

By regularly incorporating these mindful techniques into their routine, golfers cultivate a deeper awareness of their bodies, their swings, and the act of playing itself. In doing so, they unlock the potential to experience each round with renewed enthusiasm and focus. Present moment awareness is not just a practice; it is a commitment to the joy of the game—where every swing is a mindful invitation to connect with the sport and oneself fully. As we continue to explore the practical ways to integrate mindfulness into golf, you will discover the profound impact that cultivating present moment awareness can have on your performance and enjoyment of the game.

Reducing Performance Anxiety

Performance anxiety is a prevalent challenge faced by golfers, often stemming from a deep-seated fear of failure or concern over how their game will be perceived by others. This anxiety can manifest in various ways, including racing thoughts, physical tension, and heightened self-doubt, all of which can severely hinder performance on the course. In these moments of pressure, mindfulness emerges as a powerful ally, equipping golfers with effective tools to manage their emotions and regain focus.

The first step in addressing performance anxiety through mindfulness is to recognise and accept these feelings without judgment. Rather than becoming entangled in a cycle of negative thoughts, golfers are encouraged to observe their anxiety with curiosity and openness. This practice fosters a sense of detachment, creating a buffer between the golfer and their anxious thoughts. Instead of viewing anxiety as an opponent to be defeated, mindfulness teaches practitioners to acknowledge it as a natural part of the competitive experience—one that can be observed and understood.

By shifting their perspective, golfers can reduce the intensity of their anxiety and reclaim their focus on the task at hand. The practice of mindfulness empowers them to stay grounded in the present moment, allowing for a clearer mental state that is crucial during high-pressure situations. Techniques such as mindful breathing, visualisation, and body awareness serve as anchors, helping golfers cultivate a sense of calm and composure amidst external pressures.

Through mindful breathing, for example, golfers can take a moment to centre themselves, inhaling deeply to draw in focus and exhaling slowly to release tension. This conscious act of breathing can help ground them, providing clarity as they prepare to execute their shots.

In addition to breathing techniques, mindfulness encourages golfers to embrace positive visualisation, picturing each swing and shot with confidence and ease. By mentally rehearsing successful outcomes, players can actively counteract anxiety, transforming fears into a proactive focus on execution.

Ultimately, by integrating mindfulness into their practice, golfers can learn to recognise performance anxiety as a fleeting experience rather than a defining aspect of their game. This shift allows them to approach competition with greater resilience and confidence, enhancing their performance even under pressure. As we continue to explore the transformative power of mindfulness, you will see how these techniques not only reduce anxiety but also promote a more enjoyable and fulfilling golfing experience.

Building Resilience Through Mindfulness

Resilience is a vital trait for success in golf, especially when faced with setbacks or unexpected challenges on the course. The ability to bounce back from difficult situations not only enhances performance but also enriches the overall experience of playing. Mindfulness plays an essential role in fostering resilience by cultivating a growth mind-set—a transformative perspective that encourages individuals to view challenges not as insurmountable obstacles but as valuable opportunities for improvement.

When golfers encounter adversity, such as missing a crucial shot or facing unfavourable conditions, the traditional response may be frustration or discouragement. However, mindfulness offers a different approach: it allows players to acknowledge their mistakes without becoming overwhelmed by negative emotions. Instead of allowing a missed shot to define their performance or mood, golfers can learn to observe their emotions with curiosity and acceptance. This practice leads to constructive analysis, enabling them to identify what went wrong, glean valuable lessons, and move forward with intention.

This resilient mind-set shifts a player's approach to the game, transforming the experience of competition into a cycle of continuous learning. Each round becomes a journey, rich with opportunities to practice mindfulness and cultivate an attitude of curiosity. By embracing the lessons that come with mistakes, golfers can develop greater adaptability and strength, ready to face the next challenge with renewed vigour.

Moreover, mindfulness instils a sense of patience, prompting individuals to remain calm during tense moments on the course. This capacity to maintain composure under pressure is key to navigating the highs and lows of the game with grace. As golfers develop resilience through mindfulness, they become better equipped to handle adversity, allowing them to stay focused on their performance and enjoy the game even amid challenges.

Ultimately, building resilience through mindfulness empowers golfers to approach their sport with an open heart and an agile mind. By learning to embrace each experience—regardless of the outcome—they cultivate a deeper connection to the game. As we continue to explore mindfulness in subsequent chapters, we will delve into specific practices that can further enhance this resilience, equipping you with the tools to become a more adaptable and confident golfer. Embrace the transformative power of mindfulness, and watch as it cultivates resilience on the course and in every aspect of your life.

Enhancing Enjoyment of the Game

Golf is fundamentally meant to be an enjoyable experience—a unique opportunity to connect with nature, oneself, and fellow enthusiasts of the sport. Each round offers a chance to immerse oneself in the beauty of the course, revel in the rhythm of one's swings, and share moments of camaraderie with others. However, the pressure to perform can often overshadow this inherent joy, reducing golf to a series of anxieties and expectations rather than an enjoyable pursuit.

Mindfulness presents a transformative solution, reintroducing a sense of playfulness to the game. By focusing on the present moment, golfers are invited to pause and truly appreciate their surroundings. The vibrant hues of the greens, the subtle rustle of leaves, and the sound of a well-struck ball become sources of joy and inspiration. As players engage with the here and now, they rediscover the simple pleasure of the game—an experience of connection that transcends mere scores and statistics.

Practicing mindfulness allows golfers to cultivate a deep sense of gratitude for the experience of playing. This gratitude can manifest in various ways: feeling thankful for the opportunity to enjoy a sunny day on the course, appreciating the challenge and beauty of each shot, or celebrating the shared laughter and stories among friends. Such appreciation enhances the bond between the player and the sport, leading to a more fulfilling and satisfying connection.

Each game then transforms into an opportunity to be present, revel in the moment, and celebrate the sheer act of playing golf. This shift in perspective invites golfers to embrace the journey rather than fixate solely on outcomes. By recognising the joy inherent in each swing, each hole, and each interaction, players find themselves enriched by the experience, making golf not just a game, but a source of inspiration and fulfilment.

As we explore the principles and practices of mindfulness throughout this chapter, you will discover strategies to enhance your enjoyment of the game. By embracing mindfulness, you will learn to navigate the pressures of competition with grace while unlocking a deeper appreciation for the sport you love. Ultimately, let go of the need for perfection and allow yourself to enjoy the beautiful journey of golf, one mindful shot at a time.

Practical Mindfulness Techniques for the Course

To harness the transformative benefits of mindfulness on the golf course, golfers can incorporate a variety of practical techniques into their routines. These practices enable players to cultivate presence, enhance performance, and deepen their enjoyment of the game. Here are four essential mindfulness techniques that can be easily integrated into your pre-shot preparation and overall golfing experience:

1. **Mindful Breathing:** Mindful breathing serves as a fundamental technique to centre your thoughts and calm your nerves. Before each shot, taking a few moments to focus on your breath can create a calming effect, allowing you to approach the game with clarity.

   This simple yet effective practice calms the nervous system, enhances focus, and creates a centred mental state that is essential for peak performance.

2. **Body Scan Awareness**: Heightened body awareness is crucial for golfers aiming to execute a smooth swing. A body scan allows you to become more in tune with your physical sensations, promoting relaxation and fluidity in your movements.

   This practice encourages relaxation and connection with your body, leading to smoother and more controlled movements, enhancing your overall performance.

3. **Visualisation:** Visualisation is a powerful mental technique that can significantly enhance focus and build confidence. By imagining each shot before execution, golfers set the stage for success.

   This technique enhances concentration and strengthens belief in your abilities, ultimately translating into improved performance during the game.

4. **Post-Game Reflection:** Taking time to reflect on your performance after each round is essential for personal growth and development as a

golfer. This practice allows you to process your experiences, draw valuable insights, and acknowledge your progress.

This technique reinforces a growth mind-set, allowing you to recognise both successes and challenges as vital aspects of your journey as a golfer. It creates an opportunity to celebrate progress and encourage self-awareness.

Conclusion

Incorporating mindfulness into your golf game offers a profound opportunity to enhance both focus and enjoyment on the course. By developing present moment awareness, golfers can clear mental clutter and concentrate solely on the task at hand, which is crucial for executing each shot with precision. Mindfulness equips players with the tools to manage performance anxiety, encouraging them to approach challenges with a sense of curiosity and resilience.

As golfers learn to embrace mistakes as learning opportunities rather than setbacks, they foster a growth mind-set that enhances their overall experience of the game. Beyond performance, mindfulness helps rekindle the joy of playing golf, allowing individuals to appreciate the beauty of their surroundings, the rhythm of their movements, and the shared camaraderie with fellow players.

By incorporating practical techniques—such as mindful breathing, body scans, visualisation, and post-game reflections—into their routines, golfers can create a mental environment that not only supports peak performance but also enriches their connection to the sport. Ultimately, the practice of mindfulness transforms the golf course from a mere venue for competition into a place of personal growth and fulfilment. As you embark on your journey with mindfulness, may each round be an opportunity to embrace the present moment, cultivate resilience, and deepen your love for the game.

2.2: Success Stories of Professional Golfers Who Use Mindfulness

As the world of sports continues to evolve, the significance of mental health and well-being has emerged as a vital focus for athletes across disciplines. In the realm of golf, where the mental game often holds equal weight to physical skill, many professional golfers have turned to mindfulness practices as a means of elevating their performance and enhancing their overall experience of the sport.

This chapter highlights the inspiring success stories of several notable golfers who have embraced mindfulness as an integral part of their training regimen. Through their journeys, these athletes have experienced transformative effects on their performance, mind-set, and enjoyment of the game. Each story serves not only as a testament to the power of mindfulness but also as a source of encouragement for golfers at all levels seeking to improve their mental resilience and connection to their sport.

Within the narratives of these professional golfers, we will explore how mindfulness has helped them navigate high-pressure situations, manage expectations, and cultivate a sense of focus and presence during competition. We will delve into their personal experiences, revealing the specific techniques and practices they employ, whether it be mindful breathing, visualisation, or reflective journaling.

Moreover, these stories illustrate that mindfulness is not merely a tool for overcoming challenges, but a means of deepening their appreciation for golf as a lifelong journey of growth and exploration.

As we embark on these inspiring journeys, it becomes clear that the practice of mindfulness can unlock the full potential of athletes, allowing them to play with not just skill, but also joy and intention. Join us as we celebrate the successes and insights of these dedicated professionals, demonstrating how the integration of mindfulness into their game has led to lasting transformations both on and off the course.

Phil Mickelson: Mastering the Mental Game

Phil Mickelson, one of golf's most celebrated players, is renowned not only for his impressive accolades, which include multiple major championships and a storied career, but also for his unwavering commitment to mental preparation. As a player who has navigated the complexities of the professional circuit, Mickelson has openly emphasised the significance of mindfulness and visualisation techniques in enhancing his game.

Mickelson has shared insights into his practices that help him master the mental aspects of golf, illustrating how crucial it is to mentally visualise success before executing a shot. He employs mindfulness by visualising the desired outcome of each stroke. He imagines the ball's flight path, the satisfying sound it makes upon striking the target, and the feelings of accomplishment that accompany successful execution. This mental imagery is coupled with a profound awareness of his body and the environment in which he plays, allowing him to fully immerse himself in a focused state during critical moments.

These mindfulness practices enable Mickelson to enhance his ability to perform under pressure, demonstrating that mental preparation is as vital as physical skill in the world of golf. His disciplined approach to mindfulness underscores the profound impact that mental training can have on an athlete's performance, highlighting the importance of psychological strategies in achieving success in sports.

Mickelson's commitment to integrating mindfulness into his routine serves as an inspiration to golfers at all levels, exemplifying how the mental game can empower players to reach their full potential.

Source: Mickelson, Phil. "Mindful Preparation: Creating a Winning Mental Game."

Rory McIlroy: Finding Balance Through Mindfulness

Rory McIlroy, a four-time major champion and one of golf's most prominent figures, has openly shared his journey with mindfulness and the crucial role it plays in both his life and career. Faced with the pressures of fame and the intense mental toll of competitive play, McIlroy recognised the need to cultivate a more balanced approach to golf—one that would allow him to thrive amid the expectations that accompany his status as a top athlete.

In his exploration of mindfulness practices, McIlroy has embraced techniques such as meditation and breathing exercises, which have proven instrumental in helping him regain focus and mental clarity. By integrating mindfulness into his daily routine, he has developed the capacity to manage anxiety and maintain composure on the course, enabling him to concentrate on each shot without being overwhelmed by the weight of past mistakes or the fear of future outcomes.

This profound shift in mind-set has not only enhanced McIlroy's performance but has also enriched his overall enjoyment of the game. By learning to embrace the journey of golf and appreciate the present moment, he has discovered a newfound love for the sport. This perspective allows him to play with greater freedom and enjoyment, reinforcing the idea that golf is not only about results but also about the experiences and connections formed along the way.

Rory McIlroy's journey into mindfulness serves as an inspiration to golfers everywhere, showcasing how a balanced mind-set can lead to both professional success and personal fulfilment on and off the course.

Source: McIlroy, Rory. "Mindfulness in Golf: Finding Balance Under Pressure."

Annika Sörenstam: Pioneering Mindfulness in Women's Golf

Annika Sörenstam is widely regarded as one of the greatest female golfers in history, not only for her remarkable achievements on the course, which include ten major championships, but also for her innovative approach to the game. Throughout her illustrious career, Sörenstam has embraced mindfulness as a core component of her training regimen, emphasising its significance in cultivating mental strength and awareness.

Recognising that golf is as much a mental challenge as it is a physical one, Sörenstam has integrated mindfulness practices such as visualisation and deep breathing into her preparations for competition. By honing her mental focus through these techniques, she has developed the ability to maintain composure in high-pressure situations—allowing her to tap into her full potential and perform at her best when it matters most.

For instance, before stepping onto the first tee, Sörenstam might visualise the successful execution of her shots, picturing both the trajectory of the ball and the satisfaction of a well-played round. Deep breathing exercises help her centre her thoughts and reduce anxiety, grounding her in the present moment before facing the challenges of the course.

Sörenstam's commitment to mindfulness has resonated within the golfing community, serving as an inspiration for many aspiring golfers. Through her advocacy for mental preparation, she has highlighted the importance of adopting mindfulness practices in achieving success—encouraging others to explore this transformative approach to the game.

Her pioneering influence extends beyond her own career; Sörenstam has contributed to a growing movement in women's golf that emphasises the profound impact of mental health and well-being on performance. By championing mindfulness, she has paved the way for future generations of female golfers, demonstrating that a strong mental game is just as crucial as physical skill in achieving excellence in the sport.

Source: Sörenstam, Annika. "The Mental Game: How Mindfulness Transformed My Approach to Golf."

Bryson DeChambeau: The Science of Mindfulness

Bryson DeChambeau, renowned for his analytical approach to golf and exceptional physical conditioning, stands out not only for his impressive performance but also for his innovative integration of mindfulness into his training regimen. DeChambeau's commitment to the sport goes beyond traditional methods, as he employs mindfulness techniques to sharpen his focus and elevate his performance, particularly during critical moments of competition.

DeChambeau practices a form of mindfulness that involves a comprehensive mental routine before each shot. This routine is meticulously designed to connect his physical preparation with mental clarity, ensuring that both aspects of his game are in sync. As he steps up to the tee, he engages in deep breathing and visualisation exercises, fostering a sense of calm that allows him to approach each shot with intention and confidence.

By cultivating a profound awareness of his thoughts and emotions, DeChambeau has been able to minimise distractions and enhance his decision-making on the course. This heightened state of awareness enables him to process information swiftly and effectively, allowing for optimal performance during high-pressure situations. His unique blend of scientific analysis and mindfulness serves as a powerful reminder of how the mental aspect of golf can be a game-changer.

Furthermore, DeChambeau's methodical approach to mindfulness reflects his commitment to understanding the intricacies of the game. He often attributes his success to the synergy of mental strength and physical prowess, emphasising the importance of this dual approach in achieving excellence.

By incorporating mindfulness into his regimen, Bryson DeChambeau exemplifies how golfers can leverage mental practices to augment their physical abilities, demonstrating that success in the sport is as much about the mind as it is about skill. His journey highlights the evolving nature of golf, where the mental game holds significant power—a lesson that resonates with players at every level.

Source: DeChambeau, Bryson. "The Science of Golf: How Mindfulness and Analysis Merge for Peak Performance."

Zach Johnson: Cultivating a Winning Mindset

Zach Johnson, a two-time major champion with a distinguished career in professional golf, attributes a significant portion of his success to the strength of his mental game. Recognising that golf is as much about what happens between the ears as it is about technique, Johnson has embraced mindfulness as a vital practice to manage the stresses inherent in competitive play.

Through mindfulness, Johnson has cultivated a mind-set grounded in presence and awareness, enabling him to maintain unwavering focus on each shot. This focused approach prevents him from succumbing to external pressures—such as the expectations of fans and competitors—or internal doubts that can easily cloud judgment. By fostering this level of awareness, Johnson empowers himself to approach every shot with clarity and intention.

Central to Johnson's philosophy is the idea of a growth mind-set. He fundamentally believes that every experience—whether deemed positive or negative—contributes valuable lessons to his evolution as a golfer. This perspective shifts the focus from the outcome of a shot to the insights gained from the process itself. His commitment to mindfulness allows him to embrace this mind-set fully, viewing challenges as opportunities for growth rather than setbacks.

Moreover, Johnson's practice of mindfulness has instilled in him a positive outlook that translates directly into resilience and consistency on the course. This unwavering positivity helps him navigate the emotional roller coaster of professional golf, allowing him to bounce back swiftly from disappointments and maintain momentum through challenges.

Zach Johnson's journey exemplifies how cultivating a winning mind-set through mindfulness can lead to sustained success in golf. His insights serve as a powerful reminder for all players about the importance of mental strength in achieving their goals. By integrating mindfulness into your own practice, you can develop the same resilience and clarity that have defined Johnson's illustrious career.

Source: Johnson, Zach. "The Mindset of a Champion: Insights on Mindfulness and Resilience."

Lydia Ko: Embracing the Present

Lydia Ko, a two-time major champion and former world number one, has spoken openly about her commitment to mindfulness and its impact on her game. "Mindfulness allows me to stay present and focused during tournaments," Ko explains. "It helps me to let go of what has happened in the past and not worry about what's coming next. I can just focus on the shot in front of me, and that makes a significant difference."

By integrating mindfulness into her routine, Ko not only approaches her rounds with clarity but also cultivates a greater appreciation for the process of playing golf. This practice has enabled her to manage the pressures that come with being a top player while maintaining a sense of joy and purpose both on and off the course.

Source: Ko, Lydia. "Finding Peace in the Pressure: My Journey with Mindfulness."

Jason Day: Cultivating Mental Clarity

Jason Day, the Australian golfer and former world number one, has utilised mindfulness to enhance his mental resilience and maintain focus through the ups and downs of competition. "In golf, your mental state is just as important as your physical game," Day states. "Through mindfulness, I've learned to control my thoughts and stay calm, even when the stakes are high."

Day incorporates techniques such as meditation and visualisation into his practice, helping him to stay grounded and focused during tournaments. "Mindfulness allows me to enter each round with a clear mind and a positive outlook. It's about being fully engaged with the present, which translates into better performance and satisfaction with the game."

Source: Day, Jason. "The Mental Game of Golf: Mindfulness in Action."

Michelle Wie West: Harnessing Mindfulness for Balance

Michelle Wie West, a prominent figure in women's golf and a major champion, has expressed how mindfulness has helped her balance the demands of professional golf with her personal life. "Mindfulness has been a game-changer for me, both on the course and in my daily life," she notes. "It teaches me to find peace and balance, which is essential in this sport that can be so mentally taxing."

Wie West emphasises the importance of being present, particularly during competitive rounds. "It's easy to get caught up in the results and the expectations, but mindfulness helps me focus on my game and enjoy the experience. I've learned to celebrate my small victories and understand that every shot is a part of my journey."

Source: Wie West, Michelle. "Mindfulness in Golf: Finding Balance and Peace on the Course."

Paul Casey: The Mental Edge

Paul Casey, a seasoned competitor on the PGA Tour, advocates for mindfulness in enhancing performance by cultivating a strong mental edge. "I believe that mindfulness allows me to be in the moment, which is crucial in this game," Casey explains. "When you're playing under pressure, having that mental clarity is essential. Mindfulness has given me the tools to stay composed and focused, regardless of the situation."

By integrating mindfulness techniques such as deep breathing and meditation into his routine, Casey reports feeling better equipped to face the mental challenges of golf. "It helps me enter a state of flow where everything feels natural and effortless," he adds, highlighting the tangible benefits of mindfulness on his performance.

Source: Casey, Paul. "How Mindfulness Became My Competitive Advantage."

Conclusion

The success stories of professional golfers who utilise mindfulness illustrate its undeniable benefits in the world of competitive golf. From Phil Mickelson's visualisation techniques to Rory McIlroy's quest for balance, mindfulness has proven to be a powerful ally for enhancing performance, reducing stress, and fostering a love for the game.

These athletes remind us that golf, while requiring skill and precision, is equally a mental challenge. By embracing mindfulness, golfers can cultivate the awareness, focus, and resilience needed to navigate the complexities of the sport, ultimately enjoying a richer and more fulfilling experience.

As we continue our exploration of mindfulness, we will delve into practical techniques that any golfer can use to integrate these principles into their own game. Every player has the potential to harness the power of mindfulness to transform their performance, drawing inspiration from the journeys of these accomplished athletes.

Chapter 3: Mindful Practices for Golfers

Golf is not just a physical game; it is an intricate dance between the mind and body, where mental acuity and emotional resilience play crucial roles in achieving success. As golfers, we are challenged not only by the terrain and weather conditions but also by internal distractions like anxiety, negative thoughts, and the pressure to perform. This is where the integration of mindfulness can profoundly enhance our performance and overall enjoyment of the sport.

In this chapter, we will delve into specific mindful practices designed to help golfers cultivate awareness, improve focus, and foster a sense of peace on the course. Mindfulness invites us to engage fully in the present moment, allowing us to approach each shot with clarity and intention. With these practices, golfers can learn to navigate the psychological challenges of the game, transforming moments of stress into opportunities for growth.

We will explore various techniques, including mindful breathing, visualisation, body awareness, and mindful reflection, each offering unique tools to enhance both mental and physical performance. These practices not only prepare athletes for competition but also promote self-compassion and a deeper connection to their golfing experience.

As you engage with the mindful techniques presented in this chapter, consider how they can enrich not only your game but also your approach to life. Whether you are a seasoned player or just starting your journey in golf, the integration of mindfulness can lead to transformative outcomes, allowing you to embrace each round with confidence and joy. Together, let's embark on a journey of mindful practice that elevates your game and enhances your overall well-being.

3.1: Breathing Techniques to Maintain Calmness and Focus

Breathing is an involuntary act that sustains life—a fundamental function we often take for granted. Yet, within the realm of sports, particularly golf, mastering the art of breathing can profoundly impact performance and experience on the course. The breath serves as a powerful tool for cultivating calmness and focus, transforming the golfer's mental landscape into one characterised by clarity, presence, and composure.

In the dynamic environment of golf, where distractions abound and pressure can mount easily, harnessing the power of breath becomes essential. Thoughtful breathing techniques can anchor golfers in the present moment, helping to alleviate anxiety and centering the mind before tackling each shot. By integrating specific breathing practices into their routines, players can cultivate a sense of calm that enables them to engage with the game fully, enhancing their overall experience.

This chapter delves into various breathing techniques that are easily adaptable to a golfer's regimen. From conscious deep breathing to rhythmic inhalation-exhalation practices, these techniques are designed to promote relaxation and clarity amid the high demands of competition. We'll explore the science behind how breath influences our physical and mental states and provide practical exercises that can be seamlessly incorporated before, during, and after your rounds.

Through these breathing techniques, golfers can learn to manage their emotions, sharpen their focus, and optimise their performance on the course. As we dive into the world of mindful breathing, prepare to unlock a transformative aspect of your game—one that fosters not only improved performance but also a deeper sense of enjoyment and fulfilment in every round you play. Let the breath be your guide as you navigate the mental challenges of golf, allowing it to cultivate a space of calm and focus that enhances your journey in the sport.

The Science of Breathing

Before exploring specific breathing techniques, it is crucial to understand the profound impact that breath has on our mental and physical states. The body's autonomic nervous system—which regulates countless involuntary processes, including breathing—plays a pivotal role in how we respond to stress and relaxation. This system comprises two primary branches: the sympathetic nervous system, responsible for the 'fight or flight' response, and the parasympathetic nervous system, which fosters relaxation and calmness.

When golfers encounter stress or anxiety, their sympathetic nervous system often takes the lead, triggering physiological responses that prepare the body to react to perceived threats. This activation results in increased heart rates, heightened tension, and impaired focus—conditions that can significantly hinder performance on the course. However, golfers can consciously counteract this response by engaging the parasympathetic system through intentional breathing.

By harnessing the power of breath, players can evoke a state of calmness and balance, promoting clarity of thought and enhancing physical readiness. Deep, deliberate breathing activates the parasympathetic system, counteracting the body's stress response and returning it to a more harmonious state. This practice allows golfers to shift from a reactive mindset—dominated by stress and impulsivity—to a responsive one, grounded in mindfulness and presence.

Through mindful breathing, golfers create the conditions necessary for optimal performance. They can better manage the stressors of the game, maintain composure in high-pressure situations, and embrace each moment with intention and focus. Understanding the science of breathing not only empowers golfers with the knowledge of how to influence their physiological state but also provides them with a powerful tool for transforming their approach to challenges on the course.

As we delve further into the breathing techniques designed to enhance your game, keep in mind the foundational connection between breath and the body's nervous system. By aligning your breath with your mental and physical goals, you unlock the ability to perform at your best, cultivating a heightened sense of control and awareness that enriches both your golfing experience and overall well-being.

1. **Diaphragmatic Breathing:** Diaphragmatic breathing, often referred to as abdominal or deep breathing, is a foundational technique that encourages the fullest exchange of oxygen in your body—promoting a breath that is fuller, deeper, and more effective than shallow chest breathing. Unlike superficial breaths that engage the upper chest, diaphragmatic breathing utilises the diaphragm, a large muscle located at the base of the lungs, thereby engaging the core and activating the body's natural relaxation response. This practice is particularly beneficial for golfers seeking to maintain calmness and focus under pressure, as it fosters both physical relaxation and mental clarity.

Technique:

1. **Find a Comfortable Position**: Begin by finding a comfortable standing position or sit down with your back straight. This alignment facilitates the movement of the diaphragm and ensures optimal breathing.
2. **Hand Placement**: Place one hand gently on your abdomen and the other on your chest. This positioning helps you monitor the

movement of your breath and ensures you are engaging the diaphragm effectively.
3. **Inhale Deeply**: Inhale deeply through your nose, allowing your abdomen to rise and expand as you fill your lungs with air. Keep your chest relatively still, focusing on the movement in your abdomen. This indicates proper use of the diaphragm.
4. **Pause and Hold**: Hold your breath for a brief moment. This pause allows for a complete exchange of gases in the lungs and fosters concentration and focus.
5. **Exhale Slowly**: Exhale slowly and gently through your mouth, allowing your abdomen to fall naturally. Aim for a slow, controlled release, focusing on the sensation of air leaving your body and the relaxation that follows.
6. **Repeat the Cycle**: Continue this process for several cycles, concentrating on the rise and fall of your abdomen. Each breath should be a conscious, deliberate action, reinforcing the connection between body and mind.

Engaging in diaphragmatic breathing confers numerous benefits that are particularly advantageous on the golf course. This technique can help reduce physical tension, lower heart rate, and clear the mind, helping to establish a calm baseline before taking a swing. By integrating diaphragmatic breathing into your pre-shot routine, you can create a mental environment that promotes focus and composure, allowing for more consistent and effective performance. As you practice this technique, you will find that deliberate breathing becomes a natural tool for navigating the pressures of the game, transforming your approach with serenity and intention.

2. **Box Breathing:** Box breathing, also known as square breathing, is a structured and deliberate technique that incorporates equal phases of inhalation, retention, exhalation, and a second retention. This method is revered for its ability to promote focus and relaxation, making it an invaluable tool during high-pressure moments on the golf course. By engaging in box breathing, golfers can cultivate a heightened sense of calm and mental clarity, equipping them to face challenges with poise and precision.

Technique:

1. **Inhale Deeply**: Begin the cycle by inhaling deeply through your nose for a count of four (1, 2, 3, 4). Imagine filling your lungs as fully as possible, drawing in the breath with intention and care.

2. **Hold Your Breath**: Once your lungs are filled, hold your breath for a count of four (1, 2, 3, 4). During this pause, focus on the stillness and harness the moment to gather your thoughts and composure.
3. **Exhale Slowly**: Gently exhale through your mouth for a count of four (1, 2, 3, 4). Release the breath in a controlled manner, envisioning stress and tension leaving your body with each outflow.
4. **Hold Again**: Before starting the next cycle, hold your breath once more for a count of four (1, 2, 3, 4). Embrace the quiet and centeredness that this moment brings, preparing to begin the process anew.
5. **Repeat the Cycle**: Continue this rhythmic breathing pattern for several minutes, allowing its cadence to soothe your mind and anchor your focus.

The rhythmic nature of box breathing offers significant benefits for golfers, particularly in stabilising the mind and body during critical moments. This technique instils a sense of stability and control, facilitating a mental space where focus and intention thrive. By engaging in box breathing, golfers can centre themselves before pivotal shots, minimising the impact of external pressures and internal anxieties.

Box breathing serves as a bridge between breath and the present moment, allowing athletes to be wholly attentive to the task at hand. As you incorporate this powerful technique into your routine, you will discover that its calming influence enhances your ability to perform under pressure, transforming each moment on the course into an opportunity for mindful engagement and success. Embrace box breathing as a core component of your mental game, and experience the profound impact it can have on your golfing journey.

3. **The 4-7-8 Breathing Technique:** The 4-7-8 breathing technique, popularised by Dr. Andrew Weil, is a simple yet effective practice that promotes relaxation and aids in reducing anxiety. This rhythmic method not only helps oxygenate the body but also activates the parasympathetic nervous system, which is responsible for promoting a state of calm and recovery. By incorporating this technique into their routines, golfers can enhance their mental clarity and emotional resilience, paving the way for improved performance during high-pressure situations.

Technique:

1. **Find Your Position**: Begin by sitting or standing comfortably, ensuring that your back is straight. This posture facilitates optimal breathing and encourages relaxation.
2. **Inhale Quietly**: Take a deep inhalation through your nose for a count of four (1, 2, 3, 4). Focus on filling your lungs completely, allowing your abdomen to expand with each breath.
3. **Hold Your Breath**: After the inhalation, hold your breath for a count of seven (1, 2, 3, 4, 5, 6, 7). This pause creates a moment of stillness, helping centre your mind and body.
4. **Exhale Completely**: Exhale slowly and fully through your mouth, making a gentle "whoosh" sound as you release the breath for a count of eight (1, 2, 3, 4, 5, 6, 7, 8). Focus on emptying your lungs entirely, letting go of any tension or stress with the breath out.
5. **Repeat the Cycle**: Complete this breathing cycle for four full breaths, gradually increasing the number of cycles as you become more comfortable with the technique.

The unique structure of the 4-7-8 breathing technique—specifically the lengthening of the exhale relative to the inhalation—serves to calm both the mind and body. This extended exhalation encourages relaxation, helps lower heart rate, and reduces feelings of anxiety, creating a tranquil mental environment that is essential for optimal performance on the golf course.

This technique is particularly useful when facing moments of pressure, such as preparing for a crucial putt or navigating challenging course conditions. By employing 4-7-8 breathing, golfers can effectively manage their anxiety levels and restore focus, allowing them to approach each shot with clarity and confidence.

Incorporating the 4-7-8 technique into your pre-shot routine or using it as a reset during a round can significantly enhance your mental resilience, ensuring that you remain engaged in the present moment and can perform at your very best. As you practice this simple yet powerful breathing technique, you will find that it not only enriches your game but also contributes to your overall well-being.

Mindful Breathing During Play

Incorporating mindful breathing during play is an especially effective strategy for staying grounded amidst distractions and overcoming moments of doubt. Whether faced with the pressure of competition or the mental chatter that often accompanies a round of golf, mindful breathing serves as a powerful anchor, helping golfers remain present and focused. The following practical approaches can be seamlessly integrated into your golfing routine to enhance your mental state and performance on the course:

- ❖ **Pre-Shot Routine:** Before addressing the ball, take a few moments to engage in a focused breathing technique, such as diaphragmatic breathing or box breathing. This pre-shot ritual can set a tone of calmness, centre your thoughts, and enhance your focus.

Technique:

1. Stand behind the ball, visualise your target, and take a deep breath.
2. Utilise diaphragmatic breathing by inhaling deeply through your nose, allowing your abdomen to expand fully.
3. As you hold your breath for a moment, visualise success, and exhale slowly, imagining any tension or distractions leaving your body.

This ritual prepares you mentally and physically, fostering a concentrated mind-set essential for executing each shot.

- ❖ **Between Shots:** Utilise the transition time between shots to foster mindful breathing. This practice not only serves to reset your mental state but also provides an opportunity to reflect on the previous shot without becoming mired in overthinking or frustration.

Technique:

1. As you walk to your next shot, take a few deep breaths, grounding yourself in the present moment.
2. Acknowledge how you felt during your last swing, allowing the experience to inform you without dwelling on it.

3. Focus on the rhythm of your breath—inhale for a count of four, hold for two, and exhale for six—allowing each breath to clear your mind.

This practice helps maintain a clear perspective and reignites your focus on the current shot, enhancing both mental clarity and emotional resilience.

- **When Overwhelmed:** In moments when feelings of anxiety or pressure escalate during play, employing the 4-7-8 breathing technique can effectively restore composure, clearing your mind and enabling greater focus.

Technique:

1. In a discreet moment, practice the 4-7-8 technique by inhaling quietly through your nose for a count of four.
2. Hold your breath for a count of seven, allowing the stillness to envelop you.
3. Exhale slowly through your mouth, making a gentle "whoosh" sound, for a count of eight.
4. Repeat this cycle for several breaths, centering your thoughts and emotions.
5. This method calms the nervous system and lowers heart rate, helping you regain control and focus when it is needed most.

Alternate Nostril Breathing:

Alternate nostril breathing, known as Nadi Shodhana in yoga practices, is another effective technique that balances the body's energies and promotes mental clarity and calmness. This practice helps golfers ground themselves, ensuring a centred state before making their next swing.

Technique:

1. **Posture**: Sit comfortably with your back straight. Bring your right hand to your face, ready to move between nostrils.
2. **Inhale Through Left**: Use your right thumb to gently close your right nostril. Inhale deeply through your left nostril for a count of four.

3. **Close Left, Exhale Right**: Close your left nostril with your ring finger, then open the right nostril and exhale slowly through the right side for a count of four.
4. **Inhale Right**: Inhale through the right nostril for a count of four, then close it with your thumb and open the left nostril, exhaling through the left side for a count of four.
5. **Continue the Pattern**: Continue this alternating pattern for five to ten cycles, maintaining your focus on each breath and the sensations associated with it.

Alternate nostril breathing encourages relaxation, increases focus, and balances energy levels, making it an excellent choice for golfers seeking to calm their minds before a swing. By integrating this technique into your pre-shot routine, you can foster a profound sense of presence and clarity, ultimately enhancing your performance on the course.

Progressive Muscle Relaxation:

Progressive Muscle Relaxation (PMR) is a technique meticulously designed to promote both physical and mental relaxation by combining controlled breathing with the intentional tensing and relaxing of muscle groups. This practice is particularly beneficial for golfers who often experience tension that accumulates in their bodies during a round, potentially affecting their performance and enjoyment of the game.

Through PMR, golfers can learn to identify areas of tension and consciously release them, fostering a deeper sense of calm and enhancing their overall bodily awareness. This heightened awareness not only contributes to relaxation but also allows for improved fluidity and control in movement during swings.

Technique:

1. **Find Your Space**: Begin by locating a quiet space where you can sit or lie down comfortably. Ensuring that you are free from distractions will enhance your ability to focus on the practice.
2. **Establish a Calming Rhythm**: Start with a few minutes of diaphragmatic breathing to set a calming rhythm. Inhale deeply through your nose, allowing your abdomen to expand, and exhale slowly through your mouth, releasing any tension you may be holding.

3. **Start with Your Feet**: Focusing on your feet, take a deep breath in and tense the muscles in that area as you inhale, holding the tension for five seconds. Feel the strain build before moving to the next step.
4. **Release the Tension**: Exhale fully and immediately release the tension in your feet. Pay close attention to the sensation of relaxation that follows, savouring the contrast between tension and release.
5. **Progress Through the Body**: Work your way upwards through your body. Progressively tense and relax each muscle group as follows: calves, thighs, abdomen, chest, arms, shoulders, neck, and finally, your face. Take your time with each area, ensuring you maintain focus on your breath and the sensations experienced.
6. **Reflect on Your Experience**: After completing the cycle, take a few moments to notice how your body feels. Engage in mindful awareness of any residual tension that may remain, appreciating the overall effect of the relaxation practice on your physical and mental state.

The benefits of Progressive Muscle Relaxation extend well beyond immediate relaxation. PMR enhances body awareness, empowering golfers to recognise areas of unnecessary tension that may impact their swings. By fostering improved relaxation, golfers not only experience greater fluidity in their movements but also cultivate a profound sense of ease that allows them to engage with the game more fully.

Furthermore, the practice of PMR serves as a valuable tool for managing stress, both during a round and in daily life. As golfers incorporate this technique into their routines, they may discover that they can maintain composure and focus even in high-pressure situations, ultimately elevating their performance and enjoyment of the sport. Embracing Progressive Muscle Relaxation can thus lead to a holistic improvement in how you approach golf, enhancing your well-being both on and off the course.

Visualisation with Breathing

Combining visualisation with breathing techniques can create a powerful mental practice for golfers, merging the art of mental imagery with focused breath to enhance concentration and reinforce positive outcomes. This holistic approach empowers players to prepare not only physically but also mentally for the challenges they face on the course, setting the stage for improved performance and a more enjoyable experience.

Technique:

1. **Find Your Comfort Zone**: Begin by choosing a comfortable position, whether you are sitting on a bench, standing in the tee box, or even in the comfort of your home. Ensure that you are in a space where you can focus without distractions.
2. **Establish Calmness**: Initiate the process with diaphragmatic breathing to calm your mind and body. Inhale deeply through your nose, allowing your abdomen to expand fully, then exhale slowly through your mouth, releasing any tension.
3. **Visualise Success**: As you inhale deeply, begin to visualise a successful shot. Picture every detail vividly: the ball soaring through the air, your swing mechanics as they come together seamlessly, and the satisfying sound of the club making contact with the ball. Engage all your senses in this imagery, making it as real and detailed as possible.
4. **Hold the Image**: Maintain that successful image in your mind while continuing to breathe steadily for a few more breaths. Focus on how it feels to execute the shot perfectly, letting the sensation of success permeate your entire being.
5. **Release Doubts**: As you exhale, visualise any doubts or distractions leaving your body with your breath. Imagine these negative thoughts dissipating into the air, creating space for confidence and focus to take their place.
6. **Repeat the Process**: Implement this mental imagery and breathing technique before each shot, or during practice sessions to reinforce the mental connection between visualisation and execution.

The integration of visualisation with deep breathing serves multiple purposes, enhancing self-confidence and sharpening focus as golfers mentally prepare for each shot. By regularly practicing this technique, players can cultivate a strong mental framework that supports a positive mind-set. The ability to visualise success allows golfers to approach each shot with assurance, reducing anxiety associated with performance pressure.

Moreover, this technique fosters a state of relaxation, further enhancing concentration on the task at hand. As golfers begin to see and feel their desired outcomes through visualisation, they align their physical preparation with positive mental imagery, increasing the likelihood of successful performance.

Ultimately, the combination of visualisation and breathing techniques becomes an invaluable part of a golfer's toolkit, empowering them to embrace their abilities and enjoy the journey of play. By consistently applying these practices, golfers can transform their approach to the game, enhancing both their skills and their overall experience on the course.

Incorporating Breathing into Daily Practice

While the breathing techniques discussed in previous chapters hold immense value during play, their benefits extend well beyond the confines of the golf course. By incorporating these practices into your daily routine, you can reinforce a state of calmness and focus, ultimately enhancing your overall performance both on and off the course. Below are several practical avenues through which you can seamlessly weave mindful breathing into your everyday life:

1. **Morning Routine:** Start each day with a few minutes dedicated to deep breathing exercises. This intentional practice not only sets a positive tone for the day but also primes your mind and body for the challenges ahead.

Technique:

1. Upon waking, find a comfortable seated position in a quiet space.
2. Engage in diaphragmatic breathing, inhaling deeply through your nose and allowing your abdomen to rise fully.
3. As you breathe out, visualise your goals for the day—both in life and on the golf course. Picture your upcoming round: the swings you wish to perfect, the mind-set you want to maintain, and the enjoyment you aim to derive from the experience.

This morning mindfulness ritual cultivates focus, instils a sense of purpose, and enhances clarity as you navigate the day's activities.

2. **Warm-Up Practice:** Before heading to the golf course or engaging in practice sessions, dedicate time to mindful breathing exercises. This pre-game routine not only eases you into your swing but also promotes a relaxed state of mind, helping you establish a better connection with your body.

Technique:

1. Allow about 5-10 minutes before your practice to engage in focused breathing.
2. Start with slow, deep inhales, and exhale deliberately, releasing any physical tension or mental clutter.
3. With each exhale, visualise relaxation flowing through your muscles, preparing you for movement.

This mindful warm-up fosters a heightened sense of awareness, improves range of motion, and creates a calm yet focused mind-set as you transition into your practice.

3. **Cool Down:** After completing your rounds of golf or practice, take the time for thorough reflection while employing relaxation techniques. This cool-down period is essential for releasing tension accumulated during your game and preparing for the next session.

Technique:

1. Find a quiet spot to sit or lie down comfortably.
2. Engage in mindful breathing, gradually allowing your breath to return to its natural rhythm.
3. Reflect on your performance, acknowledging any successes and challenges, without dwelling on judgments. Use this time to process your experiences mentally.

By consciously unwinding and reflecting post-practice, you foster emotional resilience and enhance your ability to learn from each experience, laying the groundwork for future improvement.

Mindfulness Apps

Consider utilising mindfulness and meditation apps that feature guided breathing exercises tailored for athletes. These digital resources can be a valuable addition to your mindfulness practice, providing structured sessions that reinforce your techniques and introduce you to new methods.

Technique:

1. Download a mindfulness app of your choice, such as Headspace, Calm, or Insight Timer.

2. Explore different guided sessions focused on breathing, stress reduction, or performance enhancement.
3. Integrate these sessions into your daily routine, whether you use them in the morning, as part of your warm-up, or during breaks throughout your day.

Utilising mindfulness apps not only diversifies your practice but also provides convenience and accessibility, allowing you to engage in focused breathing wherever you are.

Conclusion

Incorporating mindful breathing techniques into your daily practice serves as a powerful foundation for enhancing both your golf game and overall well-being. By mastering various breathing practices—such as diaphragmatic breathing, box breathing, 4-7-8 breathing, alternate nostril breathing, progressive muscle relaxation, and visualisation—you equip yourself with the tools to maintain calmness and focus, significantly improving your performance and enjoyment on the course.

From starting your day with intention to unwinding after a round, each mindful breath reinforces the crucial connection between body and mind. This connection not only nurtures physical readiness but also cultivates mental clarity and emotional resilience, allowing you to manage stress and embrace the challenges of both golf and daily life with greater confidence.

As you commit to these practices, you will discover that consistency is key. Just as you dedicate time to honing your physical skills, cultivating the art of mindful breathing creates a solid foundation for a resilient and focused mind-set. By actively engaging with your breath, you open the pathway to unlocking your full potential on the golf course, enabling you to navigate each challenge with clarity, composure, and purpose.

Ultimately, mindfulness is not merely a technique but a way of being—an invitation to experience each moment with awareness and appreciation. Embrace the power of your breath as you journey through your golfing experience, and you may find that it enriches not just your game, but your entire approach to life. With every mindful breath, you enhance your connection to the sport you love, transforming your outlook and freely celebrating the unique journey of being a golfer.

3.2: Visualisation Exercises to Improve Performance

Visualisation is a powerful mental technique widely employed by athletes across various sports to enhance performance, build confidence, and prepare for competition. In the game of golf, where precision and mental acuity are paramount, the ability to clearly visualise successful outcomes is a transformative practice that can significantly impact a player's performance.

At its core, visualisation involves creating detailed mental images of desired results, allowing golfers to mentally rehearse their shots before executing them. This technique not only sharpens focus but also fosters a strong sense of self-efficacy—an essential component of success in golf. By envisioning the ball's perfect trajectory, the feel of a successful swing, and the satisfying sound of the ball making contact with the target, golfers can instil confidence in their abilities and engage with the game more fully.

This chapter delves into the fundamental principles of visualisation and its myriad benefits for golfers. We will explore how mental imagery can improve focus, boost confidence, and mentally prepare players for high-pressure situations on the course. Additionally, we will provide practical exercises designed to help you implement visualisation techniques into your routine, ensuring that you are prepared to tap into the power of mental imagery during your rounds.

By embracing visualisation as a regular practice, you give yourself the chance to create a vivid mental roadmap to success, transforming anxiety into confidence and uncertainty into clarity. As we journey through this chapter, keep in mind that visualisation is not just a tool for enhancing performance; it is a pathway to deepening your connection to the game and enriching your overall golf experience. Let us explore the principles and techniques that will enable you to harness the transformative power of visualisation, shaping you into a more focused and empowered golfer.

Understanding Visualisation

At its core, visualisation involves creating detailed mental images of desired outcomes. This technique engages the mind's eye, allowing athletes to simulate performance scenarios in a controlled and intentional manner. By imagining themselves successfully executing a shot, navigating a challenging hole, or managing pressure during a critical moment, golfers can create a mental rehearsal that prepares them for actual performance.

Research in sports psychology highlights that the brain processes imagined actions similarly to actual physical activities. When golfers visualise a swing, their brain activates the same neural pathways as if they were physically performing that swing. This connection can enhance muscular memory, develop confidence, and reduce performance anxiety.

The Benefits of Visualisation

Visualisation is a powerful technique that offers a myriad of benefits for golfers, significantly enhancing both their performance on the course and their overall mind-set. One of the foremost advantages of visualisation is **enhanced focus**. By engaging in mental imagery, golfers can concentrate on the specific aspects of their game, honing in on key techniques and precision. Through the practice of mentally rehearsing each shot, players train their minds to dismiss distractions, firmly establishing their presence in the moment. This heightened focus is invaluable when faced with the complexities of a round.

Another significant benefit of visualisation is the **increased confidence** it fosters. Imagining successful outcomes cultivates a strong sense of belief in one's abilities, reinforcing the notion that success is attainable. As golfers visualise themselves executing successful shots, they create a mind-set centred on achievement rather than fear. This shift reduces the anxiety often associated with high-pressure situations, allowing players to approach their game with greater self-assurance.

Moreover, visualisation contributes to **improved muscle memory**. By repeatedly picturing a particular swing or technique, golfers reinforce motor patterns that are essential for consistent performance. This mental rehearsal helps players integrate these movements into their muscle memory, ensuring that the physical actions become second nature during play. As a result, golfers can focus on executing their shots with the confidence that their technique is well-practised and reliable.

In addition to enhancing focus and building confidence, visualisation plays a critical role in **stress reduction**. By mentally picturing favourable outcomes, golfers create a psychological buffer against anxiety and pressure that often accompany competitive play. This positive imagery acts as a source of calmness, enabling players to approach challenges with clarity and composure. When pressure mounts, harnessing the power of visualisation allows golfers to remain centred, minimising the impact of external stressors.

Finally, visualisation aids in **strategy development**. It empowers golfers to mentally navigate the course, envisioning layouts and shot strategies well before they take the first swing. By preparing for various scenarios—considering where hazards lie, assessing distances, and identifying target zones—players can craft effective game plans that enhance their overall performance. This proactive approach allows for greater adaptability and confidence during play, as golfers feel prepared to tackle whatever challenges the course presents.

The multifaceted benefits of visualisation make it an invaluable practice for golfers. By enhancing focus, boosting confidence, improving muscle memory, reducing stress, and aiding in strategy development, visualisation equips players with the tools needed to elevate their game. As you delve deeper into the practice of visualisation, you will discover how this powerful technique can transform not only your performance but also your entire experience of the game, leading to a deeper connection and appreciation for the sport you love.

Practical Visualisation Exercises

To harness the power of visualisation for improved performance, golfers can incorporate the following exercises into their training routines:

1. **Pre-Round Visualisation** Ritual: Before each round, take a few moments to visualise the entire game. Follow these steps:
   1. Find a quiet space before heading to the course. Close your eyes and take a few deep breaths to centre yourself.
   2. Imagine yourself on the first tee, visualising the course conditions, your surroundings, and your state of mind.
   3. Picture each shot as you move through the course, visualising every detail—the swing, the ball's trajectory, how it interacts with the green and the sound of it landing perfectly.
   4. Visualise yourself calmly and confidently facing challenges, overcoming obstacles, and executing your game plan successfully.
2. **Shot-Specific Visualisation:** This exercise focuses on visualising a particular shot, allowing golfers to enhance their technique and confidence.
   1. Select a specific shot you want to improve, whether it's a drive from the tee, an approach shot to the green, or a crucial putt.
   2. Close your eyes and take deep breaths to ground yourself in the present moment. Visualise standing over the ball, feeling the grip of the club in your hands.
   3. Imagine the precise movements involved in the shot—your stance, the swing mechanics, and the follow-through.

4. Picture the ball flying through the air toward your target, feeling the sense of satisfaction as it lands exactly where you intended.
5. Repeat this visualisation several times, reinforcing the imagery and the positive emotions associated with executing the shot successfully.

3. **Course Walkthrough Visualisation:** This exercise helps golfers familiarise themselves with a course, strategising their plays.
    1. Before playing a round, spend time visualising each hole from the tee to the green. If possible, use a scorecard or course map for reference.
    2. Begin with the first hole: See yourself on the tee, analyse the layout, and visualise your club choice and aim.
    3. Imagine each shot for each hole: visualise how you will play through hazards, navigate doglegs, and approach the green.
    4. Spend time with each hole, picturing the entire sequence of shots you will take—this mental walkthrough reinforces your strategy and readying yourself for play.

4. **Reflective Visualisation Post-Round:** After completing a round, reflective visualisation can enhance learning and growth.
    1. Find a quiet moment to reflect on your play. Close your eyes and think back to specific shots or moments throughout the round.
    2. Visualise both successes and areas for improvement. Picture yourself executing successful shots again while considering what you would change in moments that didn't meet your expectations.
    3. Focus on the emotions you experienced during the round and acknowledge your progress, reinforcing positive feelings and learning from challenges.

Conclusion

Incorporating the practice of visualisation into your training routine offers a wealth of benefits that can significantly enhance both your performance on the course and your overall experience of the game. Visualisation is not merely a technique; it is a powerful mental strategy that enables golfers to cultivate detailed mental imagery, leading to improved focus, heightened confidence, and the development of essential muscle memory for consistent execution of skills.

The practice of visualisation allows players to prepare not just physically, but also mentally, equipping them with the tools necessary to navigate the challenges presented by competition. As golfers engage in this transformative process, they learn to embrace a positive and proactive mind-set. By visualising successful outcomes and addressing potential challenges in their minds, players can mitigate anxiety and cultivate resilience. This shift empowers them to transform potentially stressful situations into valuable opportunities for growth and learning.

The practical exercises outlined in this chapter are foundational for integrating visualisation into your training and competitive routines. By making visualisation a regular part of your preparation—whether through pre-round rituals or post-game reflections—you shape your experiences and outcomes on the course. Each technique serves as a pathway to greater self-awareness and enhanced performance, reinforcing the connection between mind and body.

As you continue to develop your golfing skills, remember that the mind plays a crucial role in shaping your reality. Embrace visualisation as an essential component of your practice, unlocking the potential to perform at your best with clarity, confidence, and a renewed sense of joy. Whether standing on the tee box or preparing for a critical putt, allow your imagination to guide your performance, creating a vivid mental picture of success that you can carry with you throughout every round. With intentional practice and commitment to visualisation, you not only enhance your golf game but also deepen your connection to the sport, enriching your entire experience on the course. Mindfulness and visualisation together create a transformative journey, empowering you to approach each game with optimism and enthusiasm.

3.3: Meditation Practices for Mental Clarity and Stress Reduction

In the fast-paced world of sports, where split-second decisions can determine the outcome of a game, maintaining mental clarity and emotional resilience is critical for success. Golf, while often perceived as a serene game, presents its own set of pressures and challenges. One of the most effective tools for enhancing mental strength and fostering a sense of calm is meditation. This chapter explores various meditation practices designed to improve mental clarity, reduce stress, and ultimately enhance performance on the golf course.

Understanding Meditation

Meditation is a practice deeply rooted in mindfulness and awareness. It involves focusing one's thoughts and energy to cultivate a profound state of calmness and clarity. Through techniques such as breath awareness, visualisation, and body scans, meditation encourages practitioners to observe their inner thoughts without judgment. This practice allows golfers to disconnect from distractions, alleviate anxiety, and reconnect with their true selves, enhancing their overall performance and presence on the course.

Research has shown that regular meditation practice can yield a multitude of benefits, including improved focus, heightened emotional intelligence, and increased resilience in the face of stress. By integrating meditation into their daily routines, golfers can develop a mental toolkit equipped to prepare them for various challenges, from navigating high-pressure tournament scenarios to managing self-doubt and anxiety.

In the following sections, we will explore specific meditation techniques that golfers can easily incorporate into their practice regimens. By focusing on enhancing mental clarity and reducing stress, these approaches will enable you to cultivate a deeper connection to both the game and your own state of mind. As you engage with these meditation practices, you'll find that they not only elevate your performance on the golf course but also enrich your overall quality of life, fostering a sense of mindfulness that extends well beyond the fairways.

Join me on this exploration of meditation as a foundational element of your golfing journey—a journey that promises to empower you with clarity, confidence, and an enduring sense of calm.

The Benefits of Meditation for Golfers

Meditation offers a myriad of benefits for golfers, enhancing both their performance and overall experience on the course. One of the most significant advantages is **enhanced focus**. Regular meditation trains the mind to concentrate and maintain attention on the present moment, which is invaluable for golfers as it allows them to approach each hole with precision and clarity.

Additionally, meditation promotes **stress reduction**. By fostering relaxation and alleviating the physical effects of stress, it helps golfers manage anxiety levels, enabling them to enter competitive situations with a calm and centred mind-set. As a result, they can focus on their game rather than being overwhelmed by external pressures or internal doubts.
Furthermore, meditation encourages **improved emotional regulation**. Through heightened awareness of one's thoughts and emotions, golfers can learn to respond to challenges with greater thoughtfulness, rather than impulsively reacting. This ability to navigate emotions effectively

contributes significantly to maintaining composure during high-stakes moments.

Moreover, consistent meditation practice cultivates **increased resilience**. Golfers who engage in meditation become mentally tougher, better equipped to handle the inevitable ups and downs of the game. They can bounce back more quickly from setbacks or mistakes, transforming difficult experiences into learning opportunities.

Finally, meditation fosters a **deeper connection to the game**. By developing mindfulness, golfers can cultivate a greater appreciation for the experience of playing. This allows them to immerse themselves fully in the game, connecting with both the intricacies of their performance and the beauty of the natural surroundings on the course. In essence, the practice of meditation enriches the golfing experience, promoting not only better performance but also a profound sense of joy and fulfilment.

Practical Meditation Practices

To fully harness the myriad benefits of meditation for enhancing mental clarity and reducing stress, golfers can seamlessly incorporate several practical meditation techniques into their training routines. These practices not only serve to deepen focus and bolster resilience but also create a supportive mental environment that fosters peak performance on the course. By intentionally embracing these meditation techniques, golfers can cultivate a greater sense of well-being and prepare themselves to navigate the challenges of both the game and everyday life with grace and confidence. Each technique is designed to be accessible and can be tailored to fit a golfer's individual needs, making it easy to integrate mindfulness into the fabric of their daily practice.

1. **Mindful Breathing Meditation:** Mindful breathing meditation is a foundational practice that emphasises the profound power of breath as a means to cultivate presence and awareness. By centering our focus on the rhythm of inhalation and exhalation, this technique invites us to reconnect with the present moment, grounding ourselves amidst the noise and chaos of daily life.

    As we engage in mindful breathing, we learn to observer our thoughts and emotions without attachment or judgment, nurturing a state of calm that allows for greater clarity and focus. This practice serves not only to enhance our mindfulness on the golf course, enabling us to execute each shot with intention, but also enriches our overall well-being by promoting relaxation, reducing stress, and fostering emotional resilience. Embracing mindful breathing meditation as a cornerstone of your mindfulness practice paves the way for a deeper connection to both your game and your inner self.

Technique:

1. Find a quiet space where you can sit comfortably with your back straight.
2. Close your eyes and take a few deep breaths, allowing your body to relax with each exhale.
3. Bring your attention to your breath. Notice the sensation of air entering and leaving your nostrils or the rise and fall of your abdomen.
4. If your mind begins to wander, gently guide your focus back to your breathing. Acknowledge distractions without judgment.
5. Continue this practice for 5-10 minutes, gradually increasing the duration as you become more comfortable.

This practice cultivates present-moment awareness and helps calm the mind, providing a solid foundation for deeper meditation practices.

2. **Body Scan Meditation:** Body scan meditation is a powerful practice that promotes deep relaxation and fosters awareness of bodily sensations, making it particularly beneficial for golfers seeking to release tension and connect with their physical state. By gently guiding attention through various parts of the body, this technique encourages individuals to cultivate a heightened sense of awareness, allowing them to recognise areas of strain or discomfort that may otherwise go unnoticed.

As golfers engage in body scan meditation, they develop an intimate connection with their physical selves, fostering a greater understanding of how their bodies respond to the demands of the game. This practice not only facilitates the release of accumulated tension, but it also creates a sense of ease and fluidity in movement—essential elements for executing a successful swing. By incorporating body scan meditation into their routines, golfers can enhance their overall performance, promote optimal physical function, and solidify the mind-body connection crucial for athletic success. Ultimately, this technique serves as a transformative tool, enabling players to approach the golf course with a heightened sense of awareness and relaxation, paving the way for a more enjoyable and fulfilling golfing experience.

Technique:

1. Lie down comfortably on your back or sit in a relaxed position.
2. Close your eyes and take a few deep breaths to centre yourself.
3. Begin by focusing your attention on your toes. Notice any sensations, tension, or relaxation in that area.
4. Gradually move your focus upward through your body, scanning each part—from your feet to your legs, torso, arms, and head.
5. As you observe each part, consciously relax any tension you feel, releasing it with each exhale.
6. Spend 10-15 minutes on this practice, allowing your mind and body to fully relax.

This meditation fosters awareness of physical sensations, helping golfers identify and release areas of tension that may affect their performance.

3. **Visual Meditation:** Combining visualisation with meditation is a highly effective strategy for enhancing a golfer's mental imagery skills, ultimately reinforcing positive outcomes and significantly boosting confidence. This synergistic approach allows players to engage their minds in a focused, intentional manner, creating vivid mental images of successful performances that influence both their psyche and physical execution.

Through the practice of visualisation, golfers can mentally rehearse each aspect of their game—envisioning not only the flight of the ball but also the mechanics of their swing, the feel of the club in their hands, and the emotions of achieving success. When integrated with meditation, this practice fosters a deep state of relaxation and presence, enabling golfers to immerse themselves fully in these mental scenarios. The calming effects of meditation reduce anxiety and enhance clarity, allowing individuals to visualise their successes with greater precision.

As golfers consistently engage in this combined practice, they reinforce their belief in their abilities, transcend self-doubt, and establish a winning mind-set. The mental connections formed through visualisation become ingrained in their muscle memory, enabling them to execute shots with confidence and poise on the course. Ultimately, the integration of visualisation with meditation transforms the mental preparation process, empowering golfers to approach both practice and competition with renewed vigour and enthusiasm. This holistic technique serves as a cornerstone for building not only improved performance but also a lasting enjoyment of the game itself.

Technique:

1. Find a quiet space and sit comfortably. Close your eyes and take a few deep breaths.
2. Visualise a peaceful setting, such as a favourite golf course or a tranquil natural environment.
3. As you immerse yourself in this mental image, engage all your senses; imagine the sights, sounds, and smells of the environment.
4. Shift your focus to visualising a successful shot or round of golf. Picture each detail: your stance, swing mechanics, and the ball's trajectory.

Allow yourself to feel the satisfaction of executing the shot perfectly. Hold this image for several minutes before gently returning your awareness to your breath and slowly opening your eyes.

Visual meditation cultivates confidence and reinforces successful outcomes, creating a mental framework that golfers can draw upon during actual play. This practice not only enhances focus but also aligns emotional states with desired performance.

4. **Loving-Kindness Meditation (Metta):** Loving-kindness meditation is a powerful practice that fosters compassion and positivity, both towards oneself and towards others. Rooted in the principles of kindness, compassion, and goodwill, this meditation encourages practitioners to extend warm and loving thoughts first to themselves and then to those in their lives, including loved ones, acquaintances, and even those they may have conflicts with.

   For golfers, embracing loving-kindness meditation can be particularly beneficial. By cultivating a supportive and nurturing mind-set, golfers learn to approach their game—and their experiences on and off the course—with greater empathy and understanding. This practice allows players to release self-criticism and frustration, replacing negative thoughts with affirmations of compassion and acceptance.

   As golfers engage in loving-kindness meditation, they learn to appreciate their journey and acknowledge their efforts with kindness. By fostering a sense of self-compassion, players develop resilience that enhances their emotional regulation during competitive situations, allowing them to navigate stress with grace. In moments of pressure, this nurturing mind-set empowers golfers to respond thoughtfully and positively, minimising the impact of anxiety and self-doubt.

Furthermore, extending loving-kindness to others—whether it's teammates, competitors, or even referees—supports a collaborative and uplifting atmosphere. This interconnectedness fosters strong relationships, enhances team dynamics, and encourages a sense of community within the sport.

Overall, the practice of loving-kindness meditation enriches golfers' experiences by promoting emotional health and social connections. It serves not only as a means to enhance individual performance but also as a pathway to cultivate joy, resilience, and a deeper connection to the game itself. By incorporating loving-kindness into their mindfulness routines, golfers can embrace the holistic nature of their journey, transforming challenges into opportunities for growth and connection.

Technique:

1. Sit comfortably and close your eyes. Take a few deep breaths to settle into your space.
2. Begin by directing compassionate thoughts towards yourself. Silently repeat phrases such as "May I be happy. May I be healthy. May I be safe. May I live with ease."
3. After several minutes, expand the circle of compassion. Visualise someone you care about and repeat those phrases for them: "May you be happy. May you be healthy. May you be safe. May you live with ease."
4. Continue this practice by including acquaintances, neutral individuals, and even those you may have conflicts with, gradually widening your scope to encompass all beings.
5. Spend 10-15 minutes on this meditation, allowing feelings of love and compassion to fill your heart.

Loving-kindness meditation is a transformative practice that plays a vital role in cultivating a positive mental attitude and emotional resilience. This practice emphasises the importance of fostering compassion towards oneself and others, creating a nurturing environment that encourages kindness, empathy, and understanding. For golfers, embracing loving-kindness meditation can profoundly influence their approach to competition and the game as a whole.

By integrating loving-kindness meditation into their routines, golfers learn to replace self-criticism and negative thought patterns with warmth and affection. This shift enables them to approach competition with a kinder mind-set, one that acknowledges their efforts and imperfections without harsh judgment. As a result, athletes can experience a reduction in stress and anxiety, allowing them to perform with greater confidence and poise.

Moreover, cultivating compassion towards others—be it competitors, teammates, or caddies—helps create a supportive atmosphere on the course. This sense of camaraderie not only enhances the enjoyment of the game but also fosters stronger relationships among players. By practicing loving-kindness, golfers can transform potentially high-stress situations into opportunities for connection and mutual support, promoting a positive competitive spirit.

Ultimately, loving-kindness meditation encourages golfers to embrace a holistic view of their experiences, leading to improved emotional health and greater enjoyment of the game. By nurturing a compassionate mind-set, golfers can navigate the challenges of competition with grace and resilience, further enhancing their performance and deepening their appreciation for the sport. Through this practice, individuals can find balance and joy, transforming the competitive landscape into one characterised by kindness and understanding, both towards themselves and others.

5. **Guided Meditation:** Guided meditation is a compelling practice that involves listening to a recorded or live guide who leads you through the meditation process, providing structure and support as you navigate your mindfulness journey. This format can be especially beneficial for beginners or for those seeking to explore specific themes related to golf performance, relaxation, or stress management.

    For golfers new to meditation, guided sessions offer a gentle introduction to the practice, making it easier to understand the principles of mindfulness while alleviating the uncertainty that can accompany solo meditation. With a knowledgeable guide narrating the process, practitioners are encouraged to settle into a comfortable state of mind and immerse themselves fully in the experience.

    Guided meditation sessions often focus on various aspects of mental training, from enhancing concentration and visualising successful performances to cultivating relaxation and managing stress. By addressing these themes, golfers can tailor their meditation practice to meet their unique needs, whether they are preparing for an important tournament or seeking to alleviate anxiety before a round.

The power of guided meditation lies in its ability to create a sense of community and connection, as it invites participants to share in a collective experience while fostering a safe space for personal exploration. Plus, the presence of a guiding voice offers reassurance and encouragement, helping individuals stay focused and engaged throughout the practice.

As you incorporate guided meditation into your routine, you will discover that it serves as a practical tool for enhancing not only your mental game but also your overall well-being. By embracing this approach, you can take meaningful steps toward achieving a calm, centred state of mind, ultimately empowering you to perform at your best and enjoy the game to its fullest.

Technique:

1. Find a comfortable seated or lying position. Select a guided meditation focused on performance, relaxation, or stress reduction. There are many apps and online resources available.
2. Close your eyes and centre yourself with a few deep breaths.
3. Follow the instructor's guidance, focusing on the sensations and visualisations presented during the session.
4. Allow yourself to relax and absorb the guidance, letting go of any distractions.
5. Continue for the duration of the meditation, which typically lasts anywhere from 5 to 30 minutes.

Guided meditation serves as an exceptional gateway for exploring various meditation styles and themes, offering structure and direction to practitioners at all levels. Unlike traditional meditation, where one may find themselves navigating the process alone, guided sessions provide a framework that enhances understanding and engagement. This structured approach allows individuals to immerse themselves in expertly crafted experiences tailored to cultivate relaxation and mental clarity.

Through guided meditation, practitioners are led by an experienced teacher or a calming voice that sets the tone for the session. This guidance helps to eliminate uncertainty, allowing individuals to focus entirely on their meditation practice rather than becoming preoccupied with how to proceed. As a result, these sessions can significantly deepen the practitioner's experience, inviting them to explore themes that resonate with their current needs—be it stress relief, enhanced focus, emotional healing, or athletic performance.

Moreover, the varied styles of guided meditation encompass a wide range of techniques, including visualisation, breath awareness, and mindful body scans. This diversity enables individuals to discover what resonates most with them, facilitating a personalised meditation journey. Whether seeking to improve athletic performance or simply cultivate a deeper sense of inner peace, guided meditation provides practitioners with valuable tools to navigate their mental and emotional landscapes.

Ultimately, by engaging in guided meditation, individuals foster a greater sense of relaxation and clarity, enhancing their overall well-being. This practice becomes not merely a tool for calming the mind but a pathway to deeper self-discovery and personal growth. As you explore the world of guided meditation, you will find that it opens doors to transformative experiences that enrich your life and enhance your journey toward mindfulness.

Incorporating Meditation into Your Routine

To fully reap the benefits of meditation, consistency is key. By incorporating mindful practices into your daily routine or your pre-round rituals, you can enhance your overall experience of the game and cultivate a resilient mind-set. Here are several practical tips for making meditation a regular part of your golf training:

1. **Set a Regular Time**: Establish a consistent time each day for your meditation practice, whether in the morning, during lunch, or right before bed. Consistency in timing will solidify meditation as an integral aspect of your routine, making it easier to incorporate it into your life.
2. **Create a Dedicated Space**: Designate a quiet spot for meditation that is free from distractions. Comfort is essential in this space; consider adding cushions, mats, or calming decorations to create a welcoming environment conducive to relaxation and focus.
3. **Start Small**: If you're new to meditation, begin with just a few minutes each day. Gradually increase the duration as you become more comfortable with the practice. This gentle approach helps

prevent feelings of overwhelm and encourages a sustainable routine.
4. **Use Technology Wisely**: Take advantage of meditation apps or online resources that offer guided sessions, reminders, and progress tracking. Many of these apps feature programs tailored specifically to enhance athletic performance and reduce stress, making them incredibly beneficial for golfers.
5. **Link to Golf Practice**: Experiment with blending meditation into your golf practice. For instance, consider engaging in mindful breathing exercises before heading to the driving range, or visualise your tee shots during warm-ups. Integrating mindfulness into physical training can enhance both focus and performance on the course.
6. **Be Patient and Kind to Yourself**: Recognise that meditation is a skill developing over time. If distractions arise during your practice, be gentle with yourself; acknowledge the thoughts and gently redirect your focus back to your breath or visualisation. Practicing self-compassion is a crucial aspect of your mindfulness journey.

Meditation serves as an invaluable tool for achieving mental clarity and reducing stress, particularly for golfers. By engaging in a variety of mindfulness exercises—such as mindful breathing, body scans, loving-kindness, guided sessions, and visualisations—you can enhance focus, cultivate emotional resilience, and foster a positive mind-set both on and off the course.

As the game of golf continues to demand mental acuity alongside physical prowess, off-the-course preparation becomes just as vital as practice swings. By consistently incorporating meditation into your routine, you will not only improve your performance but also enrich your overall enjoyment of the game—creating a profound connection to both the sport and yourself.

Embracing the practice of meditation opens doors to self-discovery and personal growth, allowing you to manage the challenges that accompany competitive play. With regular practice, you will likely find that your ability to remain centred amid pressure improves, enabling you to respond to challenges with greater constructiveness while deepening your enjoyment of the game.

Ultimately, meditation helps cultivate a resilient mind-set that equips you to navigate the highs and lows of golf with grace and poise. So, as you step onto the first tee or confront a daunting putt, remember the power of a calm mind and the strength that comes from within. By nurturing this mental discipline through meditation, you can transform not only your game but also your relationship with golf—turning every round into an opportunity for growth, connection, and fulfilment. Embrace the journey of meditation, and watch as it elevates your performance and enhances your overall enjoyment of the sport.

Chapter 4: Pre-Game Mindfulness Routine

The moments leading up to a round of golf are often filled with anticipation, excitement, and a dash of nerves. For many golfers, the transition from preparation to play can be overwhelming, as the mind races with thoughts of performance, past mistakes, and the weight of expectations. Establishing a pre-game mindfulness routine is essential for grounding yourself and creating a focused mind-set that allows you to perform at your best.

In this chapter, we will explore the concept of a pre-game mindfulness routine, detailing how deliberately cultivating a sense of presence can enhance your concentration, reduce anxiety, and elevate your overall experience on the course. A well-crafted routine enables you to centre your thoughts, connect with your body, and set clear intentions for the imminent challenges.

We'll discuss various techniques that form the foundation of an effective pre-game routine, including mindful breathing practices, visualisation exercises, and reflective moments of gratitude. These strategies are designed to help you cultivate a state of calm awareness, enabling you to approach each shot with clarity and confidence.

As we dive into the specifics of creating your pre-game mindfulness routine, reflect on how intention, presence, and mindful awareness can shape your experiences on and off the course. You will gain valuable insights that not only prepare you for the game ahead but also serve to enrich your overall golfing journey. Get ready to transform your approach to the tee box, ensuring each round is an opportunity for growth, connection, and enjoyment.

4.1: Warm-Up Exercises That Incorporate Mindfulness

Warm-up routines are a fundamental part of preparing for any sport, and golf is no exception. However, while traditional warm-up exercises focus primarily on physical preparation, incorporating mindfulness into these routines can elevate their effectiveness. Mindful warm-up exercises not only prepare the body for the demands of the game but also centre the mind, enhance focus, and establish a positive mental state. This chapter explores warm-up exercises that seamlessly blend physical movement with mindfulness, setting the stage for an optimal golfing experience.

The Importance of a Mindful Warm-Up

A proper warm-up serves multiple essential functions that are crucial for both physical and mental readiness on the golf course. First and foremost, warming up enhances physical readiness by gradually increasing the heart rate and promoting blood flow to the muscles. This process not only prepares the body for movement but also plays a key role in preventing injuries, ensuring that golfers are in optimal condition as they embark on their rounds.

In addition to benefiting physical preparation, a mindful warm-up significantly improves mental focus. By incorporating mindfulness into this routine, golfers can shift their attention away from the distractions of daily life and cultivate a strong presence in the moment. This mental clarity helps clear the mind of clutter, enhancing concentration—a vital asset for achieving effective performance during play.

Moreover, mindful warm-ups establish a positive mind-set, fostering a state of awareness and acceptance. Engaging in intentional movement allows golfers to cultivate a sense of clarity and calmness that can transform their experience on the course. As they focus on their bodies and the rhythm of their movements, they not only enhance their physical performance but also embrace the joy of the game.

In summary, a mindful warm-up is a holistic approach that prepares golfers comprehensively—physically, mentally, and emotionally—setting the stage for an enjoyable and successful day on the links. By recognising the importance of this preparatory ritual, golfers can establish a routine that enhances their readiness and bolsters their performance, ultimately deepening their connection to the sport.

Mindfulness in Motion: Mindful Warm-Up Exercises

The following warm-up exercises blend physical movement with mindfulness practices, allowing golfers to prepare both their bodies and minds before hitting the links.

1. **Mindful Walking:** Mindful walking is a simple yet remarkably effective practice that allows individuals to ground themselves in the present moment while gradually warming up the body. This technique invites you to engage fully with the act of walking, turning a familiar movement into an opportunity for mindfulness and heightened awareness.

As you stroll, you become acutely aware of each step, the sensation of your feet making contact with the ground, and the rhythm of your breath. With every movement, you can sense the gentle rise and fall of your body as you navigate your surroundings. This creates an engaging experience—one that not only warms up your muscles but also clears your mind of distractions.

In the context of golf, mindful walking can be particularly beneficial as a pre-round warm-up, allowing you to immerse yourself fully in the environment of the course. Whether you're walking from the parking lot to the clubhouse or between holes, this practice fosters a deeper connection with the natural beauty around you—inviting you to appreciate the sights, sounds, and sensations of the moment.

In essence, mindful walking serves as a bridge to transform each step on the course into a mindful practice, setting the tone for a focused and present golfing experience. By incorporating this technique into your routine, you can cultivate a sense of calm and clarity that enriches your overall connection to the game and enhances your performance.

Technique:

1. Find a quiet area where you can walk undisturbed, whether it's a driving range or a quiet path on the course.
2. Stand still for a moment, take a few deep breaths, and become aware of your surroundings.
3. Begin to walk slowly, paying attention to each step. Feel the ground beneath your feet as you shift your weight from one foot to the other.
4. Focus on the sensations in your legs, feet, and core as you walk. Be aware of your posture and how your body engages with each movement.
5. As you walk, notice your breath. Allow it to synchronise with your steps—inhale as you take a step forward, and exhale as you place your foot down.
6. Continue walking mindfully for 5–10 minutes, allowing your thoughts to flow naturally without attachment.

Mindful walking calms the mind, increases body awareness, and prepares you for a focused and intentional round of golf.

2. **Dynamic Stretching with Breath Awareness:** Dynamic stretching is an invigorating practice that involves moving through a series of

stretches designed to mimic the movements you will perform while golfing. This active form of stretching not only helps prepare your muscles and joints for the physical demands of the sport but also enhances the mindfulness aspect of your routine when combined with breath awareness. By incorporating intentional breathing into your dynamic stretching, you establish a deeper connection between your body and mind, fostering an optimal mental state for performance.

Technique:

1. **Find Your Stance**: Begin by standing tall with your feet hip-width apart. Take a few deep breaths to centre yourself, allowing your breath to flow naturally and comfortably as you prepare for the routine ahead.
2. **Arm Circles**: Start with arm circles. Inhale deeply as you lift your arms overhead, feeling the expansion in your chest and shoulders. Exhale as you circle your arms back down to your sides, releasing any tension. Repeat this movement for 8–10 breaths, focusing on the rhythm of your breathing and the fluidity of your motions.
3. **Trunk Twists**: Next, incorporate trunk twists. Stand with your feet shoulder-width apart, lifting both arms to shoulder height as you inhale. As you exhale, gently twist your torso to the right, engaging your core. Inhale back to centre, and then exhale as you twist to the left. Continue this sequence for 5–8 twists on each side, embracing the sensation of your spine mobilising with each twist.
4. **Leg Swings**: Transition into leg swings by holding onto a stable surface for balance. Inhale as you swing your right leg forward, feeling the stretch in your hip, then exhale as you swing it back, engaging your glutes. Continue this movement for 8–10 swings before switching to the left leg, focusing on your breath as you maintain balance.
5. **Hip Circles**: Conclude your dynamic stretching routine with hip circles. Place your hands on your hips and make slow, large circles with your hips, focusing on the movement and your breath. Complete 5 circles in each direction, allowing your body to relax and loosen through the motions.

Dynamic stretching, enhanced through breath awareness, increases blood flow to the muscles, preparing them for the physical activity ahead. This practice not only enhances flexibility and range of motion but also fosters mindfulness—calming your mind and cultivating a focused state of awareness that is essential for success on the golf course. By engaging in dynamic stretching with intentional breath, golfers set a strong foundation for their game, ensuring they enter each round feeling physically prepared and mentally centred. This synergistic approach facilitates a seamless transition into play, where both body and mind are aligned for peak performance.

3. **Mindful Swing Practice:** Mindful swing practice is an exercise specifically designed to focus on the intricacies of your golf swing while embedding mindfulness into each mechanical motion. By cultivating awareness during this crucial aspect of the game, golfers can enhance their technique and foster a deeper connection with their bodies and the club.

Technique:

1. **Select Your Spot**: Begin by finding a designated area where you can practice your swing—ideally in an open space where you have the freedom to use a club and ball. Ensure the environment is calm and free from distractions, allowing for an immersive practice experience.
2. **Assume Your Position**: Stand tall with your feet set shoulder-width apart, holding your club lightly in your hands. Close your eyes and take a few deep breaths, allowing your body to relax. Ground yourself in the moment, focusing on the sensations of the ground beneath your feet and the grip of the club in your hands.
3. **Initiate Practice Swings**: Begin your swing practice by slowly making practice swings without hitting a ball. Pay close attention to the sensations coursing through your muscles and joints as you move through the swing. Notice the way your body engages and the fluidity of each motion, embracing the rhythm of the movement.
4. **Synchronise Breath with Motion**: Inhale deeply as you take the club back, feeling the expansion in your body. Then, exhale gradually as you follow through with your swing. Focus on the synchronicity of your breath with the movement—allowing the inhalation and exhalation to guide and enhance your swing.
5. **Visualise Success**: While swinging, visualise the perfect shot. Picture the ball's trajectory as it soars through the air and imagine the satisfying sensation of solid contact. Use this mental imagery to boost your confidence and clarity, reinforcing the positive feelings associated with executing successful shots.
6. **Refine Your Awareness**: Repeat this mindful swing practice for 5–10 repetitions, paying close attention to your body movements, balance, and posture throughout each swing. If accessible,

consider using a mirror or recording your swings to gain insight into your form and technique.

Engaging in mindful swing practice hones muscle memory while promoting a focused and positive mind-set. This exercise cultivates a heightened awareness of the mechanics of your swing, allowing you to approach each shot with intention and confidence. As you integrate mindfulness into your practice, you will find that the combination of awareness, breath, and visualisation not only sharpens your skills but also deepens your connection to the game of golf itself.

By committing to this mindful approach, golfers set themselves on a path toward enhanced performance and a more fulfilling experience on the course, paving the way for growth, enjoyment, and a renewed appreciation for every swing.

4. **Breathing Exercises for Calmness:** Incorporating focused breathing exercises into your pre-game routine is a powerful way to ground yourself before starting your round. These techniques not only help ease tension but also clear your mind, setting the stage for a more centred and engaged experience on the course.

Technique:

1. **Comfortable Position**: Begin by standing or sitting comfortably, ensuring that your posture is upright yet relaxed. This position allows for optimal airflow and creates a stable foundation for your practice.
2. **Deep Inhalation**: Close your eyes and take a deep, slow breath in through your nose, counting to four as you inhale. Pay close attention to the feeling of your abdomen expanding fully with each breath. This awareness promotes a connection to your body and prepares you for relaxation.
3. **Pause and Hold**: Hold your breath for a count of four, allowing yourself to savour the stillness and calm in this moment. Embrace the sense of control and awareness that accompanies this brief pause.
4. **Controlled Exhalation**: Exhale slowly and deliberately through your mouth for a count of four, consciously releasing any tension or distractions. Envision these feelings dissipating with your breath, creating space for focus and clarity.
5. **Repeat the Cycle**: Continue this breathing cycle for several minutes, focusing entirely on your breath and the sensations it creates within your body. Allow each breath to deepen your

relaxation, encouraging your mind to settle as you prepare to step onto the course.

Engaging in this breathing exercise promotes profound relaxation and helps reduce anxiety, preparing you mentally and emotionally for the round ahead. By calming the nervous system, you can re-establish focus and clarity before teeing off, ensuring that you approach the game with a composed and centred mind-set.

Through this practice, you cultivate a sense of control and presence, equipping yourself to navigate the challenges of golf with greater ease. As you integrate focused breathing exercises into your routine, you will notice the positive impact on your performance and enjoyment of the game, setting the tone for a fulfilling experience on the course. Embrace this simple yet effective practice, and allow the power of your breath to enhance not only your golf game but also your overall well-being.

5. **Visualising Success Pre-Round:** Incorporating visualisation into your pre-round warm-up routine serves as a powerful tool for reinforcing a positive mind-set and setting the stage for optimal performance. By engaging in focused mental imagery, you can create a clear picture of success that not only enhances your confidence but also calms your nerves as you prepare to take on the challenges of the golf course.

Technique:

1. **Find Your Space**: After completing your physical warm-up, seek out a quiet space where you can sit or stand comfortably. This peaceful environment allows you to centre your thoughts and prepare for your visualisation practice.
2. **Centering Breath**: Close your eyes and take a few deep breaths, allowing your body to relax. Focus on your inhalations and exhalations, letting go of any residual tension as you ground yourself in the moment.
3. **Visualise Your Round**: Begin to visualise your upcoming round of golf in vivid detail. Picture yourself playing confidently, executing every shot with precision and grace. Envision navigating the course with ease and poise, feeling every moment as you make your way through the holes.
4. **Embrace the Feelings of Success**: As you visualise each successful shot, allow yourself to fully experience the feelings of satisfaction and accomplishment that accompany those moments.

Imagine the exhilaration of a perfectly struck drive or the calm of sinking a critical putt. Cultivate a strong sense of presence, fully immersing yourself in the joy of playing golf.

5. **Immerse in Positive Emotions**: Dedicate 5–10 minutes to this visualisation practice, letting positive emotions infuse your mind and body. As you visualise success, notice how your confidence grows and how you feel more prepared to face the day's challenges.

Engaging in visualisation fosters a deep sense of confidence and helps you mentally prepare for the challenges of the game. By picturing successful outcomes and embracing positive emotions, you significantly reduce anxiety and heighten your focus. This proactive approach equips you to tackle the pressures of competition with a composed mind-set, paving the way for a more enjoyable and successful round.

As you continuously practice visualising success before your rounds, you will find that this technique not only enhances your performance on the course but also enriches your overall relationship with the game. Visualisation becomes a powerful ally, empowering you to step up to each tee with clarity, confidence, and a sense of purpose. Embrace this practice, and let it transform your approach to golf and your experiences beyond the course. **Integrating Mindfulness into Your Warm-Up Routine**

To truly maximise the effects of mindfulness, it is beneficial to integrate these practices into a cohesive warm-up routine that prepares both your body and mind for the challenges that lie ahead on the golf course. A thoughtfully structured warm-up not only enhances physical readiness but also promotes mental clarity and emotional balance, setting the tone for an enjoyable and focused round.

Begin your routine with a few minutes of **mindful walking** to ground yourself. As you stroll, centre your thoughts on the sensations in your body and your connection to the ground beneath your feet. This gentle movement fosters presence and awareness, drawing you into the moment and preparing you for the practice ahead.

Next, transition into **dynamic stretching** that incorporates breath awareness. Engage in movements that mirror the actions you will perform while golfing, such as arm circles and trunk twists. As you stretch, synchronise your breath with each movement, creating a rhythm that enhances both flexibility and focus. This practice primes your muscles and joints, ensuring that they are warmed up and ready for action.

Following your dynamic stretches, move into **mindful swing practice**. Stand in a designated area, either on the range or at home, and practice your swings with intention. Pay close attention to the mechanics of your movement, focusing on the feel of the club and the rhythm of your body. This mindful engagement allows you to hone your technique while fostering a deeper connection to the act of swinging.

Next, perform **breathing exercises** to calm your nerves and establish a centred mental state. Utilise techniques such as diaphragmatic breathing or box breathing to regulate your breath, reduce anxiety, and prepare yourself for the round ahead. This step serves as a transition, helping to settle your mind and reinforce a focused mind-set.

Finally, conclude your warm-up with **visualisation of your successful round**. Take a moment to envision yourself playing confidently and executing each shot flawlessly. Picture the trajectory of the ball, the feeling of satisfaction with each swing, and the enjoyment of the game. This mental rehearsal not only boosts your confidence but also primes your mind for success.

By creating this structured warm-up routine that integrates mindfulness practices, you set the stage for improved performance and a deeper connection to the game. As you regularly incorporate these rituals into your preparation, you may find that not only does your performance improve, but you also cultivate a richer appreciation for your experience as a golfer. Embrace this mindful approach to your warm-up, and watch as it transforms both your game and your approach to the sport you love.

Conclusion

Incorporating mindfulness into your warm-up routine is not just beneficial; it's essential for any golfer looking to elevate both performance and enjoyment on the course. By engaging in mindful walking, dynamic stretching, swing practice, breathing exercises, and visualisation, you prepare your body physically while also cultivating mental clarity and emotional balance.

These warm-up exercises help create a strong foundation for your round, allowing you to step onto the course with confidence and focus. The combination of physical readiness and mental presence fosters a sense of calm, reducing anxiety and optimising your performance when it matters most.

As you consistently integrate these mindful practices into your pre-game routine, you will likely find that your ability to concentrate improves, your resilience in handling challenges increases, and your overall connection to the game deepens. Each round becomes more than just a competitive experience; it transforms into an opportunity for personal growth and self-discovery.

Embrace these mindful warm-up exercises as integral components of your preparation, and experience how they enhance not only your golfing skills but also your appreciation for the sport. By finding stillness in movement and purpose in breathing, you'll cultivate a holistic approach to golf that nurtures both your body and mind.

As you navigate the greens, remember that the journey to improvement is as important as the scorecard. Allow mindfulness to guide you, turning every round into a fulfilling experience worthy of your passion for golf. With practice, these techniques will not only shape you into a better golfer but will also enrich your life beyond the fairways, fostering a deeper sense of peace and presence in everything you do.

4.2: Setting Intentions and Mental Preparation Before Playing

As golfers prepare to step onto the course, the significance of mental preparation cannot be overstated. Just as athletes dedicate countless hours to physically training their bodies, the act of setting clear intentions and engaging in mental preparation plays a pivotal role in influencing both performance and the overall golfing experience. The mind is an integral part of the game, capable of elevating a player's focus and resilience, shaping the outcomes of each round.

This chapter delves into the powerful practice of intention setting, emphasising its importance in creating a positive and focused mind-set prior to play. By establishing specific intentions, golfers can align their thoughts and actions with their desired outcomes. These intentions serve as guiding principles that help navigate the challenges on the course, enabling players to focus on what truly matters in the moment rather than getting side-tracked by distractions or external pressures.

We will explore the myriad benefits of mental preparation, including enhanced concentration, reduced anxiety, and a greater sense of control over one's emotional state. Furthermore, we will discuss effective strategies for cultivating a mind-set that is not only centred and intentional but also ripe for success. Techniques such as visualisation, affirmations, and mindful breathing will be examined as methods of fostering clarity and purpose before each round.

By embracing the practice of setting intentions and engaging in mental preparation, golfers can unlock their potential and create a more enriching experience on the course. This chapter aims to equip you with the tools necessary to approach your game with confidence and intention. As you delve into the art of mental preparation, remember that each round is not merely a test of skill, but an opportunity for growth, reflection, and enjoyment of the sport you cherish. Let us embark on this journey together to discover how mindfulness and intention can transform the way you engage with your game, both before you tee off and throughout your entire golfing experience.

The Power of Setting Intentions

Setting intentions is a powerful practice that serves as a guiding principle, bringing clarity and purpose to your actions both on and off the golf course. In golf, establishing clear intentions acts as a compass, directing your focus and energy throughout your round. Unlike conventional goals, which often emphasise specific outcomes, intentions are broader and more holistic. They focus on the qualities you wish to embody during your play, such as composure, joy, and curiosity.

By setting intentions, you align your thoughts, emotions, and actions in a way that supports your desired experience. This alignment encourages a grounded mind-set, allowing you to approach each hole with a sense of purpose and intention rather than being distracted by extraneous thoughts or the pressure of competition. Whether you aim to maintain calmness, foster a sense of discovery, or prioritise the process over the score, intentions ground you in the present, enhancing your overall engagement with the game.

Benefits of Setting Intentions

Setting clear intentions during your golfing practice offers a variety of compelling benefits, with one of the most significant being **increased focus**. Clearly defined intentions direct your attention to what matters most during your round. This selective focus minimises distractions and enhances concentration, enabling you to immerse yourself fully in the experience of each shot. By maintaining this focus, you can approach the game with intent, allowing for better decision-making and execution on the course.

Additionally, establishing intentions promotes **emotional regulation**, providing a framework for effectively managing your emotions as you navigate the challenges of the game. By anchoring your mind-set in your intentions, you cultivate a sense of composure and resilience that empowers you to respond thoughtfully, even when faced with adversity. This ability to stay grounded contributes significantly to maintaining performance stability under pressure, allowing you to recover more quickly from setbacks.

Furthermore, setting intentions enhances your **enjoyment** of the game. By promoting mindfulness and presence, intentions allow you to appreciate each moment of play and elevate your connection to the course and the sport itself. This focus transforms competition into a joyful journey of exploration, enabling you to revel in the experience rather than merely striving for results.

Moreover, when your mind aligns with positive intentions, you can achieve **improved performance**. This mental alignment leads to more deliberate and fluid movements, as you execute shots with clarity and confidence. The synergy between a focused mind and purposeful action enhances your overall consistency on the course, translating to better results and a more fulfilling golfing experience.

Finally, the practice of setting intentions can foster a deeper **spiritual connection** to both the game of golf and your inner self. This process encourages a heightened sense of gratitude and awareness of the present moment, allowing you to find meaning and fulfilment in every swing and each round. As you deepen this connection, you create a more enriching and rewarding relationship with golf, one that goes beyond technique and scores, and embraces the holistic experience of the game.

By recognising and cultivating these benefits, you can transform your approach to golf through the practice of intention setting, leading to a mindful, focused, and enjoyable experience that enhances both your performance and your connection to the sport.

Setting intentions is a transformative practice that empowers golfers to navigate their challenges with greater focus, emotional stability, and enjoyment. By embracing this mindful approach, you will enhance your connection to the game, cultivating a richer golfing experience. Ultimately, the act of setting intentions allows you to play with purpose, transforming each round into an opportunity for growth and fulfilment, both on and off the course.

Practical Steps for Setting Intentions

Creating a meaningful intention is a deeply personal process that may vary from player to player. It reflects your individual values, aspirations, and the unique experiences you wish to cultivate on and off the golf course. The following steps provide a comprehensive guide to help you craft intentions that resonate with your goals, enhancing both your performance and enjoyment of the game.

1. **Reflect on Your Values:** Before formulating your intentions, take time to engage in self-reflection about what truly matters to you in golf and in life. Consider the qualities you want to embody and the experiences you wish to foster during your rounds.

   Questions to Consider:

   - What do I love most about playing golf?
   - Which aspects of my game do I want to nurture and develop?
   - How do I want to feel during my rounds?

   Engaging with these questions can provide clarity and direction as you move forward in setting your intentions.

2. **Keep It Positive and Present:** When crafting your intention, it's essential to frame it positively and focus on what you want to experience rather than what you aim to avoid. Additionally, formulating your intention in the present tense creates a sense of immediacy and realisation, reinforcing your commitment to living those intentions in the moment.

   Example Intentions:

   - "I play with joy and curiosity."
   - "I stay calm and composed with each shot."
   - "I approach each hole with focus and gratitude."

3. **Visualise Your Intentions:** Once you have articulated your intentions, it's crucial to take a moment to visualise them vividly in your mind's

eye. This practice transcends simple imagination; it involves mentally embodying the qualities you wish to bring to your game and actively engaging with that vision. Close your eyes and create a detailed mental image of yourself on the course, confidently executing your shots and embodying the mind-set you aspire to achieve.

Visualise the feeling of each swing, the rhythm of your movements, and the clarity in your thoughts as you respond to challenges with poise. Picture yourself embracing each moment with joy, fully immersed in the experience of playing golf. Allow this visualisation to soak into your consciousness, reinforcing a sense of assurance and readiness. This mental rehearsal not only enhances focus but also prepares your mind and body to approach the course with confidence.

4. **Write It Down:** There is an undeniable power in putting your intentions into writing. This simple act serves as a tangible reminder of your commitment to those intentions, helping to solidify them in your mind. Consider maintaining a dedicated notebook where you jot down your intentions before every round. In this notebook, you can reflect on your goals, track your progress, and revisit your aspirations at any time.

Additionally, you might choose to create a visual representation of your intentions, such as a vision board. This creative display can capture the essence of your golfing aspirations and serve as a source of inspiration. By surrounding yourself with images and affirmations that reflect your goals, you reinforce your vision and cultivate a mind-set attuned to success.

5. **Create a Pre-Round Ritual:** To fully integrate the practice of setting intentions into your golfing routine, consider establishing a pre-round ritual that prepares both your mind and body to engage with the game. This ritual can include a harmonious blend of deep breathing, visualisation exercises, and affirmations, creating a comprehensive framework for mental readiness.

Determine a specific time and place to centre yourself before your game begins. This could be moments before stepping onto the first tee or a quiet corner of the clubhouse. Engage in deep breathing exercises to tranquilise your mind and ground your focus. Follow this with a session of visualisation, allowing your intentions to manifest in your mind. Conclude your ritual with positive affirmations, reinforcing your belief in yourself and your commitment to play with purpose.

By cultivating this pre-round ritual, you create a sanctuary of calm that allows you to transition into a focused state for the challenges ahead. This structured approach not only enhances your performance on the course but also deepens your overall experience as a golfer, inviting joy and presence into each moment of play. Embrace the power of intention setting as part of your unique pre-round ceremonial, and witness how it transforms your approach to the game.

Mental Preparation Techniques:

In addition to setting intentions, employing mental preparation techniques can greatly enhance your readiness for the round ahead. These practices help establish a focused and resilient mind-set, enabling you to navigate the challenges of the game with confidence and clarity. Below are several effective techniques that you can incorporate into your pre-round routine:

1. **Mindful Breathing:** Engaging in mindful breathing before your round is a vital practice for calming the nervous system and centering your thoughts.

   Practice:

   - Begin by finding a quiet spot where you won't be disturbed. Close your eyes and take a few deep breaths to settle into the moment.
   - Inhale deeply through your nose, allowing your abdomen to expand fully. Hold this breath for a brief moment.
   - Exhale slowly through your mouth, letting go of any tension or lingering thoughts.
   - Focus intently on your breath, allowing any distractions to drift away with each exhalation.

   This simple yet potent technique primes your mind for the challenges that await, fostering a state of mindfulness that enhances your performance.

2. **Visualisation:** Visualisation techniques serve as a powerful mental rehearsal, preparing you for your round by allowing you to picture successful shots, navigate potential challenges, and fully enjoy the game.

Practice:

- Set aside a few quiet moments to visualise your upcoming round. Close your eyes and picture yourself on the first tee, feeling confident and prepared.
- Visualise each shot, from the initial stance to the successful execution, considering how you will tackle obstacles and enjoy your time on the course.
- Embrace the positive emotions associated with success, allowing this imagery to fill you with confidence and excitement.

By mentally rehearsing your performance, you create a roadmap for success that reduces anxiety and sharpens focus.

3. **Positive Affirmations:** Creating a set of positive affirmations is an effective way to reinforce your intentions and bolster your self-confidence. These affirmations serve as reminders of your capabilities and aspirations, promoting a positive mind-set.

Practice:

- Write down a list of affirmations tailored to your goals. Examples include:
- "I trust in my ability to perform well today."
- "I am fully present, engaged, and enjoying every moment of the game."
- Recite these affirmations confidently before your round, allowing each one to resonate within you.

This practice cultivates self-belief and aligns your thoughts with your intentions, reinforcing a mind-set focused on success and enjoyment.

4. **Sensory Awareness Practice:** Taking time to engage your senses before heading to the first tee helps deepen your connection to the present moment and enhances your awareness of your environment.

Practice:

- Stand still for a moment, close your eyes, and take a few deep breaths to centre yourself.

- Open your eyes and observe the world around you. Take note of the colours, shapes, and movements in your surroundings, fully immersing yourself in the visual tapestry of the course.
- Focus on the sounds around you—whether it's the rustling of leaves, the echo of clubs, or the chatter of fellow golfers—allowing these auditory cues to ground you in the moment.
- Pay attention to the temperature and feel of the air on your skin, as well as the scent of freshly cut grass or earth that surrounds you.

Engaging your senses fosters a sense of calm and presence, preparing you for an immersive and enjoyable round.

5. **Stretch and Energise:** Incorporating gentle stretching or mindful movement into your pre-round routine helps awaken your body and release any tension accumulated from previous plays.

Practice:

- Find an open space where you can stretch comfortably. Stand or sit in a relaxed position to begin.
- Start with a few gentle neck rolls, moving slowly and mindfully to release any stiffness.
- Transition into shoulder rolls, allowing your shoulders to relax, followed by dynamic stretches that focus on your arms and legs.
- Finish with a series of trunk twists to promote mobility in your spine, engaging your core as you move.
- During each stretch, maintain awareness of your breath, inhaling deeply as you reach or move and exhaling steadily as you release tension.

By engaging your body mindfully, you not only prepare physically but also cultivate a sense of readiness that enhances your overall golfing experience.

Putting It All Together: Your Pre-Round Routine

As you prepare for your game, it is essential to craft a comprehensive pre-round routine that seamlessly incorporates intention setting and mental preparation. By thoughtfully structuring your routine, you can cultivate a focused mind-set and enhance your performance on the course.

Begin your routine by **arriving early** to the course. Giving yourself ample time before your tee time ensures that you avoid the stress of feeling rushed, allowing you to settle into the environment and mentally prepare for the round ahead.

Next, engage in **mindful breathing** for about five minutes. This practice will help centre your thoughts and calm any nerves that may arise. By focusing on your breath, you create a tranquil mental state that sets a positive tone for the challenges ahead.

Once you've taken time to breathe, **set your intentions**. Reflect on your core values and craft clear intentions for the round. If possible, write these intentions down to solidify your commitment and provide a tangible reminder of your goals throughout the game.

Following this, dedicate a few minutes to **visualisation**. Picture yourself successfully navigating the course, vividly imagining every shot and embodying the qualities associated with your intentions—confidence, focus, and joy. By mentally rehearsing your performance, you prepare your mind for the experience ahead.

Next, engage in **positive affirmations**. Recite uplifting statements that reinforce your mind-set and boost your confidence. Phrases like "I trust in my abilities" or "I am fully present and ready to play" serve as powerful reminders of your strengths and potential.

As you continue your pre-round practice, incorporate **sensory awareness** to deepen your connection with your surroundings. Take a moment to engage your senses, observing the colours, textures, and sounds that make up the beauty of the course. Acknowledge the atmosphere around you and appreciate the opportunity to play in such a serene environment.

Before taking to the course, engage in **gentle stretching**. Perform dynamic stretches to warm up your body, integrating mindful movements with your breath. This practice not only enhances your physical readiness but also cultivates a sense of fluidity and awareness within your body as you prepare to swing.

Finally, as you approach the first tee, take one last deep breath and remind yourself of your intentions. Embrace a calm and focused mind-set as you step into the round ahead. This comprehensive pre-round routine not only empowers you to approach each shot with clarity but also strengthens your overall connection to the game, allowing you to enjoy the experience to its fullest.

By dedicating time to this structured pre-round routine, you set a tone of intention and mindfulness that can enhance your performance and enrich your experience on the golf course. Embrace these practices, and watch as they transform your approach to the game, fostering both growth and enjoyment with every swing.

Conclusion

Incorporating mental preparation techniques into your pre-round routine lays a strong foundation for achieving optimal performance on the golf course. Practices such as mindful breathing, visualisation, positive affirmations, sensory awareness, and stretching are essential tools for nurturing a focused and resilient mind-set. These techniques empower you to embrace the challenges of the game with clarity and confidence, enhancing the overall experience of play.

Setting intentions plays a pivotal role in this preparation process. By fostering clarity and purpose through intentional goal-setting, you align your thoughts, emotions, and actions, creating a centred mind-set that significantly enhances focus and resilience. This alignment enables you to engage more deeply with each moment on the course, transforming every round into an opportunity for both improvement in your golfing skills and personal growth.

As you implement these mindfulness practices into your routine, remember that each round of golf is not just a test of your abilities; it is a journey of self-discovery and exploration. Embrace the moments of challenge and triumph with awareness and intention, and you will experience the transformative power of a focused mind combined with a strong sense of purpose in your game.

By approaching your play with a clear intention, you will not only enhance your performance but also cultivate a richer, more fulfilling connection to the sport. This mindful approach fosters joy and appreciation every time you tee off, allowing you to celebrate your golfing journey as a holistic experience. As you continue to embrace these mental preparation techniques, you unlock the potential for profound transformations in both your game and your overall life, making golf not just a sport, but a pathway to personal growth and fulfilment.

Chapter 5: Mindful Strategies During Play

Golf is often described as a mental game, where the ability to focus and remain composed under pressure can make all the difference between a good round and a great one. As you step onto the course, each shot brings its own set of challenges, temptations, and opportunities for distraction. In this environment, cultivating mindfulness becomes imperative for maintaining clarity, composure, and confidence.

In this chapter, we will explore mindful strategies that can be employed during play, equipping you with practical tools to enhance your performance and enjoyment on the course. These strategies focus on bringing awareness to your thoughts, emotions, and physical sensations in real-time, allowing you to respond thoughtfully rather than react impulsively.

From pre-shot routines that centre your focus to moments of mindfulness before executing a critical putt, we will discuss techniques that support staying present amidst the challenges of the game. Additionally, you'll learn how to manage stress and distractions, transforming pressure-laden situations into opportunities for mindfulness and growth.

As you navigate the intricacies of each hole, these mindful strategies will serve as your guiding principles, enabling you to approach the game with a fresh perspective—one that allows you to appreciate the journey rather than fixate solely on the outcomes. Each swing, putt, and chip will become an invitation to practice awareness and intention.

By integrating these mindful strategies into your play, you will not only improve your performance but also deepen your love for the game, transforming each round into a valuable opportunity for reflection and joy. Join us as we uncover the powerful impact of mindfulness during play and discover how it can elevate your golfing experience to new heights.

5.1: Staying Present: Techniques to Focus on the Current Shot

In the game of golf, the ability to stay present and focused on the current shot is often the key differentiator between success and failure. Each swing, putt, and chip presents a unique opportunity to make an impact on your performance, yet mental distractions—from lingering thoughts of past mistakes to anxieties about future outcomes, as well as external pressures—

can easily cloud a golfer's mind. Recognising and combating these distractions is essential for cultivating a focused and resilient mind-set.

This chapter delves into effective techniques designed to assist golfers in remaining fully immersed in the present moment, thereby enhancing focus and overall performance during every round. By adopting these mindful practices, you will learn how to navigate the mental clutter that often accompanies the sport, allowing you to engage deeply with each shot and experience.

We will explore a range of strategies, from establishing pre-shot routines to employing mindful breathing techniques and visualisation exercises. Each technique serves as a practical tool to anchor your awareness in the here and now, helping you to filter out distractions and centre your thoughts on the task at hand.

Ultimately, by mastering the art of staying present on the course, you can cultivate a deeper connection to your game and experience the enjoyment and satisfaction that comes with each shot played. Embrace these techniques, and discover how the power of presence can transform your golfing experience, leading you toward both improved performance and a richer appreciation for the sport you love. The journey begins with learning to focus, and each moment spent on the course becomes an opportunity for growth, connection, and fulfilment.

The Importance of Staying Present

Staying present on the golf course is pivotal to achieving optimal performance and enjoyment of the game. It entails fully immersing yourself in each shot and experiencing it without distraction, fostering a deep connection to the sport. When golfers manage to remain in the moment, they open themselves to a richer engagement with the game, allowing them to effectively regulate their thoughts, emotions, and physical actions.

By cultivating present-moment awareness, players can transform their approach to the game. This heightened focus not only improves concentration but also enhances decision-making processes, enabling golfers to execute their shots with greater precision. Additionally, remaining present helps in managing the inevitable emotional fluctuations that accompany competitive play, leading to a balanced response to challenges—whether it be a difficult lie or a crucial putt.

The practice of staying present instils a profound sense of control and clarity in golfers. When the mind is anchored in the here and now, players gain the ability to respond to situations with resilience and confidence, rather than becoming overwhelmed by external pressures or internal doubts. This state of mindfulness not only contributes to improved performance on the course but also deepens the overall experience of the game.

In essence, staying present is not merely a mental exercise; it is a way to honour the sport and yourself as a player. By embracing the present moment, you empower yourself to navigate the complexities of golf with greater ease, transforming each round into an opportunity for growth, reflection, and enjoyment. The journey toward mindfulness on the course begins with the practice of being fully present, allowing every swing, every shot, and every moment to resonate meaningfully in your athletic journey.

Techniques to Cultivate Present-Moment Awareness

To enhance your ability to stay present and focused on the current shot, there are several effective techniques that golfers can integrate into their practice. Each technique fosters mindfulness, allowing players to engage fully with their game and navigate the challenges of golf with greater ease.

1. **Mindful Pre-Shot Routine**: Establishing a mindful pre-shot routine is one of the most effective ways to ground yourself before executing a shot. This routine acts as a mental cue, enabling you to transition your focus from distractions to the task at hand. As you approach your ball, take a moment to breathe deeply and exhale slowly, anchoring yourself in the present. Visualise the shot you want to execute, imagining the path of the ball, your swing mechanics, and the desired outcome. Engage your senses as you feel the grip of the club, notice your stance, and listen attentively to the sounds around you. Clearly outline your target and commit to it, recognising that this moment is the only one that matters. Execute your shot with intention and awareness, allowing your body and mind to flow together harmoniously.

2. **Breath Awareness**: Practicing breath awareness is a simple yet powerful technique that can bring your mind into the present moment. Your breath is a constant companion and serves as a solid anchor for your thoughts. Before you begin your swing, take a few deliberate breaths—inhale deeply through your nose, allowing your abdomen to expand fully. Exhale smoothly through your mouth, consciously releasing any tension or distractions. With each inhalation, draw in focus and clarity, while each exhalation releases any lingering tension.

As you settle into your stance, allow your breath to guide you and keep your attention anchored on the rhythm of your breathing.

3. **Single-Tasking Focus**: In an era where multitasking has become the norm, adopting a single-tasking approach is essential for enhancing presence and performance in golf. Rather than juggling multiple thoughts or fixating on outcomes, consciously redirect your energy toward the singular task of executing your shot. As you prepare to swing, eliminate any secondary thoughts related to past performances, score, or external pressures. Concentrate solely on the shot before you—focus on the club, the ball, and your target. Set a specific intention for that shot, such as "I commit to a smooth and controlled swing," and repeat this mantra in your mind as you align yourself, reinforcing your commitment to the present moment.

4. **Engaging the Senses**: Your senses can be powerful allies in anchoring your attention and enhancing your awareness of the present moment. Engaging your senses fosters a deeper connection to the game and allows you to occupy each moment fully. Before taking your shot, take a moment to consciously attune your senses. Notice the feeling of the grass under your feet, the texture of the club grip, and the warmth of the sun on your skin. Listen attentively to the ambient sounds around you—the rustle of leaves, the chirping of birds, or the sound of clubs hitting the ball. Pay attention to the landscape before you—the colours of the trees, the contours of the fairway, and the positioning of the pin. By immersing yourself in these sensory experiences, you enhance your connection to the moment and enrich your overall golfing experience.

5. **Positive Self-Talk**: The narrative we construct in our minds can dramatically influence our ability to stay present and focused during play. By fostering a positive inner dialogue, golfers can cultivate the confidence and calmness needed for optimal focus. Before approaching your shot, consciously replace any negative or distracting thoughts with affirmations that reinforce your intention to stay focused. Use phrases such as, "I am focused on this shot," "I have prepared for this moment," or "I trust my swing." Reciting these affirmations softly to yourself as you set up for the shot allows the words to resonate, instilling a sense of calm and assurance. Ensure that your self-talk is encouraging rather than critical; if a negative thought arises, acknowledge it without judgment, gently replacing it with a positive affirmation. Reinforce this practice by reminding yourself of past successes and the preparation that has led you to this moment.

6. **Acceptance of the Present Moment**: Learning to accept the present moment—regardless of its outcomes or difficulties—enhances your ability to focus better on your shots. Acceptance creates space for clarity and concentration, allowing golfers to let go of judgments and regrets. As you prepare for your shot, acknowledge the emotions and thoughts that arise. Instead of attempting to suppress these feelings, simply observe and accept them as they come. Approach your shot with an open mind, recognising that while you cannot control the outcome, you can control your response to the situation. Remind yourself that each shot is an opportunity to learn and grow; whether executed perfectly or not, consider each swing as part of your journey, maintaining a sense of curiosity about the process.

Creating a Personal Practice

To effectively incorporate mindfulness techniques into your golf game, it's essential to create a personalised practice routine that resonates with your individual style and needs. A well-structured routine not only fosters focus and presence but also cultivates a deeper connection to the game. Here's a suggested framework to help you stay grounded and mindful during your rounds.

Begin your routine with a **warm-up** that includes gentle dynamic stretches and mindful movement. This initial phase is crucial for cultivating awareness of your body and breath. As you engage in stretching exercises, pay attention to the sensations within your muscles and joints, allowing yourself to become attuned to your physical state. This practice not only prepares your body for the demands of the game but also sets a mindful tone for the day ahead.

Next, take a moment to **set your intentions** before stepping onto the first tee. This is an opportunity to articulate the qualities you wish to embody during your round. Consider questions such as, "What mind-set do I want to bring to my game today?" and "How do I want to feel on the course?" Writing your intentions down or committing them to memory serves as a powerful reminder of your goals and aspirations, helping to anchor your focus throughout the round.

As you approach each shot, it's important to **implement a consistent pre-shot routine**. This ritual is designed to anchor your focus and prepare your mind for the task at hand. Integrate techniques such as mindful breathing, sensory engagement, and visualisation into this routine. Engaging in deep breaths can calm the nervous system, while vividly picturing your intended shot allows you to mentally prepare for success.

During your round, consciously practice **single-tasking**. This means shifting your mind-set to focus exclusively on the shot you are about to take. By letting go of distractions—such as score, past performances, or external pressures—you can immerse yourself fully in the moment. This single-focused attention enhances your engagement and execution, allowing each swing to be performed with intention.

Additionally, **reinforce positive self-talk** as you play. Use affirmations to encourage yourself and cultivate a confident mind-set. Phrases such as "I trust my abilities" or "I am focused on this moment" act as reinforcing reminders that help sustain mental clarity and emotional stability. Remember that the words you choose to speak to yourself carry immense power; speaking kindly and supportively can greatly influence your performance and mind-set.

Finally, **reflect and accept** after each hole. Take a moment to acknowledge your experiences, celebrating what went well while also recognising areas for improvement. This process is not meant to be a source of self-judgment but rather a valuable learning tool. By embracing both successes and challenges with the same openness, you foster a growth mind-set that promotes continuous learning and development.

By weaving these elements into your personal practice routine, you enhance your ability to stay present and focused, ultimately enriching your golfing experience. This mindful approach not only sharpens your skills but also deepens your connection to the game, allowing you to approach each round with a newfound sense of purpose, joy, and fulfilment. Embrace this journey of personal practice, and watch as it transforms your experience on the course into one that is both rewarding and profound.

Conclusion

Staying present and focused on the current shot is a skill that can be cultivated and strengthened through deliberate practice. By utilising techniques such as mindful pre-shot routines, breath awareness, sensory engagement, positive self-talk, and acceptance, golfers can enhance their ability to immerse themselves in the moment.

The journey of becoming more present on the golf course is not simply about improving performance; it's about deepening your experience of the game and cultivating a deeper appreciation for each swing, each hole, and each moment. When you learn to stay focused on the current shot, you not only elevate your performance but also enhance your overall enjoyment of golf.

Embrace these techniques as part of your routine and observe how they transform your approach to the game. Each shot becomes an opportunity to engage fully with the present, nurturing not only your skills as a golfer but also your connection to the sport and to yourself. As you step up to your next shot, remember: the only shot that truly matters is the one you're about to take.

5.2: Handling Pressure and High-Stress Situations Mindfully

Golf is a sport that frequently immerses its players in high-pressure situations, where the stakes can feel immense. Whether facing a critical putt to secure victory, grappling with the frustration that follows a series of missed shots, or contending with the weight of expectations—often self-imposed—the mental landscape can quickly become overwhelming. Effectively learning to manage pressure through mindfulness is essential for athletes aiming to perform at their best when it matters most.

In this chapter, we will explore a range of effective mindfulness techniques specifically designed to help golfers navigate high-stress scenarios with poise and clarity. By embracing these strategies, players can cultivate a sense of composure that allows them to remain focused on the task at hand, irrespective of the external pressures they face.

We will discuss mindful breathing techniques that can ground you in moments of anxiety, visualisations that foster confidence, and self-compassion exercises that promote emotional resilience. These practices not only empower golfers to respond thoughtfully to challenges but also equip them with the mental tools necessary to shift their perspective in the heat of competition.

As we delve into these techniques, you'll discover the transformative power of mindfulness in handling pressure situations, enabling you to maintain clarity and composure during your rounds. With consistent practice, these strategies will help reinforce your ability to face obstacles with confidence, enriching not only your performance but also your overall connection to the game. As you learn to embrace these mindful approaches, you will find that stress and pressure become manageable companions on your golfing journey, paving the way for a more fulfilling and successful experience.

Understanding Pressure in Golf

Pressure can manifest in numerous ways during a round of golf, creating unique challenges for players as they navigate the course. It often presents itself as heightened anxiety and self-doubt, which can trigger physical tension and lead to erratic performance. Recognising how pressure affects your mental and physical state is the first critical step toward managing it effectively.

Various sources contribute to this pressure, with external expectations being one significant factor. Performance pressures imposed by coaches, peers, or the competitive environment can weigh heavily on a golfer's psyche, leading to stress that distracts from focus and execution. The desire to meet these expectations can create an overwhelming burden that hinders performance.

Internal expectations form another layer of pressure, stemming from the aspirations we place on ourselves. Often influenced by previous performances or personal goals, these internal judgments can amplify anxiety and self-doubt, making it difficult to maintain a clear and focused mind-set during play. Many golfers grapple with the urge to prove themselves, which can cloud their enjoyment of the game.

Additionally, the competitive stakes of a given round play a crucial role in shaping the experience of pressure. Whether in a friendly game among friends or during a critical tournament where every shot counts, the context of the competition can elevate stress levels. The heightened stakes can transform an enjoyable round into a source of anxiety, impacting both performance and overall enjoyment.

By deeply understanding the nature of pressure and its various sources, golfers can begin to develop strategies for addressing it in a conscious and constructive manner. This awareness not only empowers players to combat anxiety but also cultivates resilience, enabling them to navigate challenges with confidence and clarity. As we explore techniques to manage pressure in the following chapters, you will discover how to transform these experiences into opportunities for growth, enhancing your connection to the game and improving your performance under stress.

Mindful Techniques for Managing Pressure

When faced with pressure and high-stress situations on the golf course, incorporating mindfulness techniques can be invaluable in maintaining composure and enhancing performance. One particularly effective method is the use of grounding techniques, which serve to bring your focus back to the present moment, allowing you to reconnect with your body and surroundings amidst the stress.

1. **Grounding Techniques:** Grounding techniques act as a powerful tool for centering yourself when feelings of overwhelm arise. By taking a moment to pause and reconnect, you can navigate the pressures of competition with greater ease.

Technique:

> Begin by recognising when you start to feel overwhelmed. Take a moment to pause; stand still and plant your feet firmly on the ground. Feel the solidity of the earth beneath you, allowing it to ground you in the present.
>
> Next, take three deep breaths, consciously experiencing each inhalation and exhalation. As you inhale deeply, visualise drawing in calm and focus; with each exhalation, let go of tension and worry. Allow your body to relax further with every breath, creating a sense of ease and clarity.
>
> Now, engage your senses to deepen your connection with your environment. Notice the texture of the grass beneath your feet, feeling every blade as it caresses your soles. Feel the weight of the club in your hands, allowing it to remind you of your purpose. Listen attentively to the ambient sounds around you—the rustling of leaves, the distant chatter of fellow players, or the gentle breeze.
>
> Finally, focus on your connection to the ground, reminding yourself that you are in control of this moment. Acknowledge the sensations you are experiencing while affirming your ability to manage the situation at hand.
>
> Utilising grounding techniques helps mitigate anxiety, reduce physical tension, and re-establish mental clarity by anchoring you firmly in the present moment. This practice serves as a reminder that, regardless of external pressures, you have the power to influence your mental state and respond thoughtfully to the challenges before you. By incorporating these mindful techniques into your routine, you can navigate high-pressure situations with grace, enhancing your performance and enjoyment of the game.

2. **Mindful Visualisation:** Mindful visualisation stands out as a powerful tool during high-pressure situations on the golf course. By vividly imagining a successful outcome, golfers can cultivate a sense of confidence and significantly reduce anxiety. This mental practice allows you to create a detailed roadmap for your performance, shaping not only your approach to the shot but also your emotional landscape.

Technique:

1. **Preparation for High-Stress Moments**: Before a crucial moment arises—be it a critical putt or a decisive drive—take a moment to engage in visualisation. Ground yourself and allow for clarity in your mind, consciously setting the stage for success.
2. **Visualising Confidence**: Picture yourself confidently approaching the shot. Envision your posture, your grip, and the serene focus in your eyes. Feel the calmness enveloping you, forming a protective shield against any distractions or pressures you may face.
3. **Detailed Imagery**: As you visualise, immerse yourself in the complete process of execution. Imagine every detail—from your stance and swing mechanics to the ball's path and its landing spot on the green. The more vivid and detailed your mental imagery, the more effective the visualisation will be.
4. **Embrace Positive Emotions**: Allow yourself to fully experience the positive emotions that come with success. Picture the relief that washes over you as the ball rolls toward its target, the joy of executing a well-planned shot, and the confidence that blooms within you. This emotional connection reinforces the mental imagery and enhances your overall experience.

The practice of mindful visualisation cultivates a positive mind-set and prepares you mentally for success. By routinely visualising your performances and the desired outcomes, you reduce anxiety about potential pitfalls, allowing a more focused and composed demeanour during play. This technique not only sharpens your concentration but also instils a sense of assurance that bolsters your overall performance.

Embracing mindful visualisation as part of your mental preparation permits you to approach each shot with clarity and confidence, transforming high-pressure situations into opportunities for success. As you incorporate this powerful practice into your routine, you will find that your ability to handle challenges improves, ultimately enriching your experience of the game and deepening your connection to the sport you love.

3. **Centered Breathing:** Centered breathing is an invaluable technique designed to help regulate your physiological response to stress, promoting a state of calmness and mental clarity. In the high-pressure environment of golf, maintaining control over your breath can serve as a formidable asset, allowing you to anchor your thoughts and emotions as you prepare for each shot.

Technique:

1. **Focus on Your Breath**: In moments of high stress, redirect your attention toward your breath. Inhale deeply through your nose for a count of four, allowing your abdomen to expand fully as you fill your lungs with air. This deep inhalation initiates the relaxation response in your body.
2. **Pause and Hold**: After taking in the air, hold your breath for a brief moment. Embrace this moment of stillness, allowing yourself to cultivate a sense of presence and focus.
3. **Slow Exhalation**: Exhale slowly and smoothly through your mouth for a count of six, consciously releasing any tension or negativity with each breath. Picture the stress ebbing away as you let go.
4. **Visualise Calmness**: As you breathe, imagine inhaling calmness and confidence, envisioning these positive feelings filling your body. Conversely, visualise your anxiety and doubt leaving with every exhalation, creating a mental landscape of clarity and self-assuredness.

The practice of centred breathing significantly reduces physical tension and stabilises your heart rate, making it easier to enter each shot with a clear and focused mind. By consciously controlling your breath, you manage the body's stress response effectively, allowing for greater emotional regulation and composure.

Incorporating centred breathing into your routine equips you with a practical tool for navigating the challenges of competition and fosters a resilient mental state that enhances performance. As you develop consistency in this practice, you will discover that calmness and clarity become second nature, empowering you to approach each round of golf with enhanced focus and confidence. Embrace the power of your breath, and allow it to guide you toward a more centred and fulfilling experience on the course.

4. **Positive Affirmations:** Harnessing the power of positive self-talk through affirmations can serve as a vital tool for bolstering your confidence and resilience, especially in high-pressure situations on the golf course. By consciously choosing to cultivate a positive inner dialogue, golfers can reset their mental frameworks, allowing for enhanced performance and satisfaction regardless of the circumstances.

Technique:

1. **Identify Empowering Affirmations**: Before facing a challenging moment—be it a crucial putt, a difficult lie, or any situation that may induce anxiety—repeat affirmations that reinforce your confidence and ability to handle pressure. Embrace statements such as "I am capable and prepared" or "I trust my skills and instincts." These affirmations serve as powerful reminders of your preparedness and strength.
2. **Create a Personal Affirmation List**: Take the time to write down a list of affirmations that resonate deeply with you. Tailor these statements to reflect your values and aspirations, ensuring they inspire positivity and empowerment. Revisit this list during practice sessions and before your rounds, allowing the affirmations to reinforce your commitment to a positive mind-set.
3. **Recite with Conviction**: When you find yourself in high-pressure situations, silently or aloud recite your affirmations, instilling them with conviction and intent. As you embody these statements, visualise yourself performing successfully, allowing your confidence to grow and your resolve to strengthen.

By incorporating positive affirmations into your routine, you actively combat negative thought patterns that can plague your mind, especially during competitive play. These affirmations promote a reassuring narrative that reinforces your capabilities, enhancing your mental fortitude in the face of stress.

Moreover, frequent engagement with positive self-talk cultivates a resilient mind-set, empowering you to navigate the challenges of golf with grace and confidence. As you integrate this practice into your training, you will find that your ability to face pressure situations transforms, leading to improved performance and a more enjoyable experience on the course. Embrace the power of positive affirmations, and allow them to guide you towards your peak potential both in golf and in life.

5. **Acceptance and Letting Go:** Mindfulness teaches us the vital art of embracing acceptance rather than succumbing to resistance. In the high-pressure world of golf, acknowledging the feelings of stress and anxiety without judgment fosters emotional resilience and empowers athletes to perform more effectively. Rather than battling against uncomfortable emotions, mindfulness encourages golfers to recognise and accept these feelings as natural components of the competitive experience.

Technique:

1. **Recognise Your Feelings**: As you prepare for your round, take a moment to notice any feelings of pressure or anxiety as they arise. Observe these emotions without labelling them as "good" or "bad." This practice of observation allows you to develop an awareness of your emotional state without becoming entangled in it.
2. **Embrace Acceptance**: Allow yourself to accept these feelings, understanding that they are a normal part of being a competitive athlete. You might internally reassure yourself by saying, "It's okay to feel nervous; I can handle this." This acknowledgment serves as a gentle reminder that experiencing these emotions is part of the journey.
3. **Practice Letting Go**: After acknowledging your feelings, engage in a practice of letting go. Visualise these emotions as clouds drifting across the sky or leaves floating down a serene stream. With each exhalation, imagine sending those feelings away from your body, creating mental and emotional space for calmness and clarity.
4. **Shift Your Focus**: Redirect your attention to your commitment to the process of the game rather than fixating on the outcome. Remind yourself that the experience of playing, learning, and growing is what truly matters. By embracing this mind-set, you foster a more enriching and fulfilling approach to golf.

The practice of acceptance and letting go significantly reduces the grip of anxiety, enabling you to move forward more freely and confidently. By recognising and accepting your feelings without judgment, you clear mental space to engage fully in the moment. This newfound clarity empowers golfers to respond thoughtfully to the challenges presented during a round, enhancing their emotional resilience and overall performance.

As you integrate the principles of acceptance and letting go into your mindfulness routine, you will find that your connection to the game deepens. You approach each round with a greater sense of peace, understanding that every shot is an opportunity for learning and growth. Ultimately, this mindful practice not only nurtures your game but also enriches your experience of life itself—teaching you to embrace each moment with grace and awareness.

Creating a Pressure Management Routine

To effectively handle pressure and high-stress situations on the golf course, establishing a personalised routine that incorporates mindfulness techniques can be immensely beneficial. This well-structured routine not only enhances your readiness to face challenges head-on but also empowers you to navigate the inevitable pressures of the game with greater ease and confidence. Here's a suggested framework to help you cultivate a robust pressure management routine.

Begin with **pre-round mindfulness**. Before stepping onto the course, dedicate a few minutes to engaging in mindful breathing or grounding exercises. This practice helps set a calm tone for what lies ahead, allowing you to enter the round with a centred and focused mind-set. Through techniques like diaphragmatic breathing, you can calm your nervous system and prepare mentally for the challenges of your game.

Next, take the time to **identify key situations** that tend to elevate your stress levels during play. Whether it's a critical shot over water, a crucial putt that could clinch a competition, or the pressure of competing in a major tournament, recognising these triggers is essential. Acknowledge these moments and prepare a strategy for each scenario, equipping yourself with the mental tools to handle them effectively as they arise.

Visualisation plays a significant role at this stage. For every identified high-pressure situation, dedicate time to picturing your successful execution. Visualise the entire sequence, from feeling relaxed and composed to performing the shot flawlessly. Envision the ball flying through the air, landing precisely where you intended, and experiencing the satisfaction of executing your plan perfectly. This mental rehearsal not only boosts your confidence but prepares your mind for the real situation.

To further bolster your preparedness, incorporate **positive affirmations** into your routine. Create affirmations specifically designed for high-stress scenarios, such as "I remain calm and focused during every shot" or "I trust my abilities to navigate any challenge." Reciting these affirmations before your round and prior to individual shots helps to reinforce your confidence and cultivate a resilient mind-set.

Another essential component is to practice **acceptance**. Embrace the understanding that feeling pressure is a natural part of being a golfer. Remind yourself that it is entirely acceptable to experience these emotions and that they do not define your performance. This acceptance allows you to approach high-stakes situations with a sense of curiosity rather than apprehension, transforming pressure into an ally rather than an adversary.

Finally, after completing your round, engage in **post-round reflection**. Take time to contemplate your performance under pressure, evaluating what worked well and identifying any challenges that arose. This reflective practice not only enhances your self-awareness but also allows you to appreciate your growth as a golfer. Recognising the progress you've made, regardless of the outcomes, fosters a positive mind-set and establishes a foundation for continuous development.

By implementing a personalised pressure management routine that incorporates these mindful practices, you equip yourself with the tools necessary to thrive in the face of challenges. This commitment to mindfulness allows you to approach your game with clarity and resilience, enhancing not only your performance but also your overall enjoyment of golf. Embrace this journey and watch as you transform the pressures of competition into opportunities for growth and connection to the sport.

Conclusion

Handling pressure and high-stress situations mindfully is essential for any golfer seeking to perform at their peak. By applying techniques such as grounding, mindful visualisation, centred breathing, positive affirmations, and acceptance, you can better navigate the inevitable challenges of the game.

Mindfulness allows you to transform pressure into a tool for growth rather than a source of anxiety. When you cultivate a present-focused mind-set, you empower yourself to approach each shot with confidence and clarity, regardless of the circumstances surrounding it.

As you implement these mindfulness techniques into your practice, remember that golf is about more than just performance; it's about embracing the journey, learning from each experience, and enjoying every moment on the course. By equipping yourself with the tools to handle pressure, you not only improve your game but also deepen your love for the sport.

So, the next time you find yourself facing a high-stress moment on the course, draw upon these techniques to ground yourself, refocus your energy, and navigate the challenge with poise. Each round is an opportunity to practice mindfulness and stay present, allowing you to play with greater enjoyment, creativity, and success.

Chapter 6: Post-Game Reflection

As the final putt drops and the round comes to a close, golfers are often left with a whirlwind of emotions: triumph, disappointment, satisfaction, and everything in between. However, the moments immediately following a game present a unique opportunity for growth and insight. Post-game reflection allows players to step back from the scorecard and connect with their experiences on a deeper level, fostering a mindful approach to learning and personal development.

In this chapter, we will explore the significance of post-game reflection as an essential component of a golfer's journey. Reflecting mindfully after a round can help you find clarity amidst the chaos, allowing you to analyse both your successes and challenges without the weight of judgment. It's an opportunity to acknowledge the effort invested in each shot, assess your mental and emotional state throughout the game, and celebrate the progress you've made.

We will delve into various techniques for effective post-game reflection, including journaling prompts, guided mindful sessions, and structured learning cycles. Each of these practices encourages you to embrace the lessons learned and draw upon them as you grow as a player.

Additionally, we will discuss the importance of self-compassion in this process. Understanding that golf, like life, is filled with ups and downs is key to developing resilience and maintaining motivation. Through mindful reflection, you can transform perceived setbacks into powerful opportunities for growth.

As you embark on this journey of post-game reflection, you'll discover that every round is a valuable teacher—both on and off the course. By cultivating a practice of thoughtful reflection, you not only enhance your performance but also deepen your appreciation for the rich tapestry of experiences that golf offers. Together, let us embrace the power of mindfulness in reflecting on your games, leading to a more rewarding and fulfilling golf journey.

6.1: Techniques for Reflecting on Your Game Without Judgment

Reflection serves as a powerful tool for growth in any sport, and golf is no exception. It provides players with the opportunity to analyse their performance, identify areas for improvement, and celebrate their successes along the way. However, the process of reflection can often become a double-edged sword. When self-judgment creeps in, it can cloud the learning process and hinder personal development.

This chapter seeks to explore mindful techniques for reflecting on your game without judgment, establishing a framework that promotes personal growth and fosters a deeper understanding of your golfing journey. Mindful reflection invites you to engage with your experiences objectively, allowing for a constructive examination of both your strengths and areas for development.

By practicing non-judgmental reflection, you create a safe space to acknowledge your emotions and experiences without the burden of self-criticism. This approach empowers you to glean valuable insights from each round, transforming perceived setbacks into opportunities for learning and empowering you to cultivate resilience.

Throughout this chapter, we will delve into various reflective practices, including journaling prompts, guided meditation, and structured analysis of your performances. Each technique is designed to encourage self-awareness and clarity, enabling you to approach your reflections with curiosity rather than judgment.

As you embrace these techniques, you will discover that reflection becomes not only a pathway to improvement but also a means of deepening your connection to the game itself. By incorporating mindful reflection into your routine, you will enhance both your skills as a golfer and your overall experience, transforming each round into a valuable journey of growth and self-discovery.

The Importance of Reflection

Reflection plays a pivotal role in a golfer's development, serving several key purposes that contribute to both performance improvement and personal growth. One of the most significant aspects of reflection is the opportunity to **learn from experience**. By carefully analysing your performance, you can gain valuable insights into what worked well during your round and what areas need improvement. This analysis is not merely focused on the score but encompasses every facet of your play—from your swing mechanics to your strategic decisions on the course.

In addition to fostering understanding, reflection allows you to set **future goals** that are realistic and achievable, guiding your practice efforts effectively. By evaluating past performances, you can identify specific skills and techniques you wish to develop further, creating a roadmap for your training. This purposeful approach ensures you remain focused on your growth, as each round becomes a learning experience that informs your future practice sessions.

Moreover, reflection contributes to **building resilience** as golfers learn to view challenges and setbacks without harsh judgment. Embracing a growth mind-set enables you to see adversity as an opportunity for learning rather than a source of frustration. By understanding that mistakes are a natural part of the game, you cultivate resilience and adaptability, both of which are essential for success in golf.

Finally, reflection enhances your overall **enjoyment** of the game. Taking time to appreciate each aspect of playing golf—whether it's navigating a challenging hole or celebrating a well-executed shot—deepens your connection to the sport. This intentional reflection nurtures a sense of gratitude for the experience, transforming competitive play into a journey filled with joy and discovery.

Despite these numerous benefits, many golfers struggle with self-criticism during the reflection process, which can hinder growth and dampen enjoyment. To cultivate a healthy and constructive approach, it's essential to implement judgment-free techniques that allow you to engage with your experiences openly. By embracing a mind-set of curiosity and self-compassion, you can transform reflection into a powerful tool for personal development, enabling you to find fulfilment and satisfaction in every round of golf.

Techniques for Reflecting Mindfully

Mindful reflection is a vital practice that fosters personal growth and development as a golfer, allowing you to learn from your experiences while minimising the pitfalls of self-judgment. The following techniques are designed to help you establish a mindful reflection practice that emphasises constructive insights and encourages a positive approach to your progress on the course.

By integrating these techniques into your post-round routine, you can cultivate a deeper understanding of your performance, reinforce your successes, and transform challenges into valuable learning opportunities. Embracing a mindful approach to reflection not only enhances your skills but also enriches your overall enjoyment of the game. Let's explore these effective strategies that will guide you on your journey of self-discovery and improvement in the world of golf.

1. **Create a Post-Round Journal:** Keeping a post-round journal serves as a dedicated space for reflection, providing a valuable opportunity to articulate your thoughts and feelings about your performance on the golf course. This practice encourages a deeper exploration of your experiences, fostering self-awareness and clarity as you review each round.

Technique:

To begin your journaling practice, set aside some time after each round to sit quietly with your journal. Find a comfortable space where you can focus without distractions, allowing your mind to settle on the reflections you wish to capture.

Start by writing about the overall experience of your round, encompassing both the highlights and low points. Reflect on the feeling of every shot, considering the physical sensations as well as your emotional state during play. What moments stood out to you? How did you feel after making a great shot or grappling with a challenging hole?

It's important to avoid fixating solely on scores. Instead, write about your enjoyment of the game, the atmosphere of the course, and the interactions you had with fellow golfers. These elements contribute significantly to the golfing experience and are worthy of recognition in your reflections.

To guide your reflections, consider using prompts such as "What went well today?" or "What am I proud of?" These questions encourage positive thinking and help cultivate a gratitude mind-set, allowing you to identify the aspects of your game and experiences that bring you joy.

Engaging in journaling promotes clarity and self-awareness, providing you with an outlet to express your thoughts freely. This practice diminishes the likelihood of negative judgments about your performance, as it encourages a balanced view of your experiences. By documenting both successes and areas for improvement, you create a roadmap for growth that validates your progress and motivates you to continue striving for excellence.

Ultimately, a post-round journal cultivates a rich narrative of your golfing journey, allowing you to celebrate your achievements while learning from your challenges. Embrace this practice as a powerful tool in your mindfulness routine, and watch as it deepens your connection to the game and enhances your overall development as a golfer.

2. **Utilise a "Learning Cycle" Framework:** Implementing a structured reflection framework can significantly enhance your ability to process experiences and keep your thoughts constructive. One effective model for this is the "Learning Cycle," which provides a simple yet powerful structure that encourages reflection through observation, analysis, and application. By engaging with this framework, you can transform your experiences on the course into meaningful insights that inform your growth as a golfer.

Technique:

1. **Observation**: Begin your reflection by writing down what occurred during your round. Focus on factual statements rather than subjective judgments. For instance, note the number of fairways you hit or missed, the quality of your putting, and the overall strategies you employed throughout the game. This clear, objective record forms the foundation for your reflection.
2. **Analysis**: Once you've captured your observations, take time to analyse the data. Consider why certain shots were successful and why others faltered. Reflect on the factors—such as technique, environmental conditions, or mental state—that contributed to these outcomes. Look for patterns in your performance but do so without labelling them as "bad" or "good." This non-judgmental perspective challenges you to understand your game more deeply, opening up avenues for growth.
3. **Application**: Based on your observations and analysis, identify one or two specific areas you would like to focus on during your upcoming practice sessions. Develop actionable strategies that will support your growth in these areas. This might involve setting targeted drills, seeking feedback from peers or coaches, or dedicating time to enhance certain aspects of your game.

This structured approach encourages a constructive reflection process, guiding you toward actionable insights while minimising self-criticism. By systematically observing, analysing, and applying what you've learned, you foster a growth-oriented mind-set that empowers you to embrace both successes and challenges as integral components of your development.

The Learning Cycle not only nurtures self-awareness but also enhances your overall golfing experience—transforming each round into a vital learning opportunity. By incorporating this framework into your post-game reflections, you set the stage for continuous improvement and a deeper connection to the game. Ultimately, this practice helps to cultivate resilience, clarity, and a purposeful approach to both your training and competitive play.

3. **Practice Self-Compassion:** Self-compassion is an essential pillar of judgment-free reflection, serving as a vital counterbalance to the self-criticism that often arises in the world of competitive golf. At its core, self-compassion involves treating oneself with kindness, understanding, and empathy, particularly during moments of difficulty and disappointment. By embracing this practice, golfers can foster a more nurturing relationship with themselves, ultimately enhancing both their performance and overall enjoyment of the game.

Technique:

1. **Frame Your Thoughts with Kindness**: When reflecting on your performance, consciously adopt a self-compassionate perspective. Acknowledge that every golfer—regardless of skill level—experiences ups and downs, and recognise that making mistakes is a natural and invaluable part of the learning process. Instead of viewing errors as failures, reframe them as opportunities for growth and understanding.
2. **Cultivate a Compassionate Inner Dialogue**: If you find yourself slipping into a critical mind-set, pause and ask yourself: "How would I respond to a friend in this situation?" This shift in perspective allows you to approach your reflections with greater empathy and kindness. Imagine offering encouragement and support to a fellow golfer; now, extend that same grace to yourself.
3. **Incorporate Affirmations of Self-Acceptance**: To reinforce self-compassion within your reflection practice, integrate affirmations that promote self-acceptance. Consider powerful statements such as "I am learning and growing as a golfer" or "Each experience is an opportunity for growth." Reciting these affirmations regularly nurtures a positive mind-set and cultivates resilience in the face of challenges.

By practicing self-compassion, you create a safe space for reflection, allowing you to acknowledge challenges and setbacks without the dark cloud of harsh judgment. This approach not only enhances your self-esteem but also contributes to emotional resilience. Instead of becoming disheartened by mistakes, you learn to respond with understanding and resolve, fostering a healthier relationship with your golfing journey.

In essence, cultivating self-compassion is about embracing your humanity as a golfer. It encourages you to acknowledge your feelings, learn from your experiences, and approach the game with a sense of kindness and patience. As you integrate self-compassion into your practice, you will find that it enriches both your skills and your overall enjoyment of the sport, transforming each round into an opportunity for growth and connection. Embrace this practice as it empowers you to navigate the complexities of golf with grace, resilience, and unwavering self-support.

4. **Focus on Process Over Outcomes:** Shifting your focus from outcomes—such as scores, wins, and losses—to the process, which encompasses techniques, strategies, and experiences, transforms the way you approach the game of golf. This mindful perspective fosters reflection that is centred on growth, allowing you to cultivate long-term improvement rather than getting caught up in the fluctuations of immediate results.

Technique:

1. **Reflect After Your Round**: After completing your round, take a moment to consider the key aspects of your playing process rather than fixating solely on the final score. Reflect on your course management decisions, the mental strategies you employed, and the swing adjustments you experimented with during the game. This broader perspective helps you appreciate the intricacies of your performance and the effort you put into your game.
2. **Document Your Learnings**: Take time to write down one or two valuable insights you gained about your approach to the course, your mental state during play, or specific techniques you implemented. Capture these reflections in your journal as a way to review your experiences meaningfully. This practice encourages self-awareness and reinforces lessons that can be applied in future rounds.
3. **Embrace Gradual Improvement**: Understand that true improvement often emerges from gradual adjustments to your process rather than immediate outcomes. Acknowledge that mastery in golf is cultivated over time through consistent effort, reflection, and adaptation. Reiterate this mind-set during your

reflections, affirming your commitment to growth rather than perfection.

Focusing on the process significantly reduces the pressure and anxiety that often accompany concerns about scores and outcomes. This shift in mentality encourages a healthier reflection practice that emphasises learning and growth over self-criticism or disappointment. By embracing this approach, you can cultivate a more enjoyable and fulfilling journey in golf, as you allow yourself to engage with the game more fully.

Ultimately, concentrating on the process empowers you to appreciate the nuances of improvement, fostering a deeper connection to both the sport and your personal journey as a golfer. As you continue to integrate this practice into your routine, you will find that your performance and enjoyment of the game flourish, transforming each round into an opportunity for self-discovery and development. Embrace the philosophy of focusing on the process, and watch as it enriches your experience on the course.

5. **Use Mindfulness Meditation for Reflection:** Mindfulness meditation serves as an effective tool for processing your experiences on the course while allowing you to detach from judgmental thoughts. By engaging in this practice, you create space to observe your experiences with a sense of curiosity and openness, which can be transformative for your growth as a golfer.

Technique:

1. **Set Aside Time for Reflection**: After completing your round, dedicate 10-15 minutes to engage in mindfulness meditation. Seek out a quiet space where you can sit comfortably and without distraction, creating a serene environment conducive to reflection.
2. **Centre Yourself**: Close your eyes and take a few deep breaths to help centre your mind and body. Feel each inhalation expand your lungs and each exhalation release tension, allowing yourself to transition into a relaxed state conducive to introspection.
3. **Bring Your Experiences to Mind**: As you continue to breathe deeply, gradually bring your attention to your experiences from the round. Observe your thoughts as they arise, highlighting both the moments of success and any setbacks you encountered. Importantly, do so without attaching labels or judgments; simply acknowledge these thoughts for what they are.

4. **Acknowledge Critical Thoughts**: Should critical thoughts emerge, treat them gently. Acknowledge their presence but allow them to pass without dwelling on them, much like clouds drifting across the sky. Redirect your focus back to your breath and your overall experience, fostering an atmosphere of acceptance for everything that unfolded during your play.
5. **Capture Insights Post-Meditation**: After your meditation, take a moment to write down any insights or reflections that emerged during the practice. Documenting these thoughts will solidify your learnings and serve as a valuable reference point for future rounds.

Engaging in mindfulness meditation for reflection encourages a thorough exploration of your feelings and thoughts while mitigating the impact of self-criticism. This practice fosters a more compassionate and constructive approach to reflection, promoting emotional resilience and helping you learn more effectively from your experiences on the course.

Ultimately, this technique empowers you to scrutinise your performance without the burden of harsh judgments, encouraging a holistic and nurturing mind-set. By incorporating mindfulness meditation into your post-game routine, you reinforce your journey of self-discovery, self-acceptance, and growth as a golfer, paving the way for continued improvement and a deeper appreciation for the game. Embrace this enriching practice, and allow it to transform your reflections into pathways of learning and connection.

6. **Engage in Peer Reflection:** Engaging in peer reflection is a powerful practice that can significantly enrich your reflection process and offer fresh perspectives on your game. Sharing experiences with fellow golfers facilitates honest conversations about the challenges and successes encountered on the course, while promoting accountability and camaraderie within the golfing community. This collaborative approach to reflection not only enhances personal growth but also fosters a supportive environment where individuals thrive together.

Technique:

1. **Create a Gathering Space**: After completing a round, gather with your fellow golfers in a comfortable setting to discuss your experiences. This could be in the clubhouse, at a local café, or even in a quiet corner of the course. The goal is to establish a safe, judgment-free environment where everyone feels encouraged to share openly.

2. **Share Highlights and Challenges**: Take turns discussing the moments that stood out during the round. Focus on both the successes and the areas for improvement. This balanced approach helps you view your performance through a comprehensive lens, acknowledging the achievements while also recognising opportunities for growth.
3. **Encourage Supportive Feedback**: Foster a spirit of collaboration by encouraging supportive feedback among peers. Highlight each other's strengths, celebrating the aspects of your games that were executed well. Discussing challenges collectively reinforces a sense of solidarity, reminding everyone that they are not alone in their struggles and that learning is a shared journey.
4. **Learn from Your Peers**: Reflect on how your fellow golfers handled similar pressure situations during the round. Consider adopting strategies that they found effective, incorporating their insights into your own practice. This exchange of ideas not only broadens your perspective but also enhances your toolkit for coping with challenges on the course.

Engaging in peer reflection nurtures a sense of community among golfers, reinforcing the idea that learning and growth are collective processes. This practice provides diverse viewpoints and shared experiences that can deepen your understanding of not only your own game but also of the myriad approaches others take.

Moreover, participating in this reflective dialogue helps to break down barriers between players, fostering friendships and support networks that enrich the overall golfing experience. As you engage in peer reflection, you will find that you not only enhance your skills but also build lasting connections within the golfing community. Embrace this practice as a vital component of your growth, and allow it to transform your journey as a golfer, making each round an opportunity for shared learning and camaraderie.

Creating Your Reflection Routine

To effectively implement the mindfulness techniques discussed, it is essential to develop a structured reflection routine tailored to your personal preferences and needs. A well-defined routine not only enhances your ability to learn from each round but also deepens your connection to the game. Below is a suggested outline for creating a comprehensive reflection routine that allows you to process your experiences meaningfully.

Immediate Post-Round Reflection

Begin your reflection journey immediately after completing your round. Spend a few quiet moments jotting down your initial thoughts and feelings about the experience. This practice should remain informal and spontaneous, serving as an unfiltered outlet for your emotions. Capture the highlights of your game, any standout moments, and your emotional state as you played. This immediate reflection helps ground your experience in the moment, ensuring your impressions are fresh and authentic.

Post-Round Journal Entry

Later in the day or during the evening, revisit your initial reflections and expand them into a more structured journal entry. Use this time to reflect on key moments from your round, carefully considering both the positive aspects and the challenges you faced. Applying the "Learning Cycle" framework can provide a clear structure for your reflections, as you move through observation, analysis, and application. This approach allows for deeper insights, transforming your experiences into actionable lessons for future rounds.

Mindfulness Meditation

Setting aside dedicated time for mindfulness meditation is an invaluable addition to your reflection routine. Engage in a session where you practice observation and curiosity toward your performance without imposing judgment. This meditative practice creates a serene mental space, enabling you to acknowledge your experiences and emotions openly. By fostering a sense of inner calm, you enhance your ability to learn from your reflections with a clear and focused mind.

Analyse Process vs. Outcome

In your reflective practice, emphasise the distinction between process and outcome. Regularly assess your focus on the techniques and strategies employed during play, rather than solely fixating on scores and results. Engage in discussions with your golf coach or trusted peers to evaluate your growth in this area. This collaborative reflection reinforces the importance of developing your skills and mind-set, fostering continual improvement and self-awareness.

Incorporate Peer Reflection

Integrating peer reflection into your routine enriches your learning experience and provides valuable insights. Engage in conversations with fellow golfers about your games, exchanging thoughts, insights, and strategies for improvement. Sharing your challenges and successes with a supportive community fosters accountability and camaraderie, transforming the reflective process into a shared journey of growth.

Celebrate Wins

Finally, make it a habit to celebrate your successes, no matter how small they may seem. Acknowledge improvements, breakthroughs, or moments when you embodied your intentions—whether that means executing a perfect swing, maintaining composure under pressure, or simply enjoying the game. By reinforcing these positive feelings attached to your growth, you cultivate an uplifting perspective that inspires continued development and engagement with the sport.

By creating a structured reflection routine that incorporates these elements, you not only enhance your capacity to learn from each round but also deepen your appreciation for the game of golf. Embrace this approach as a vital part of your practice, and watch how it transforms your experiences and performance, leading you toward a more fulfilling and rewarding golfing journey. As you commit to reflecting mindfully, you empower yourself to grow, evolve, and embrace every moment spent on the course.

Conclusion

Reflecting on your game without judgment is essential for personal development and enjoyment of golf. By employing techniques such as post-round journaling, structured learning cycles, self-compassion, a focus on process, mindfulness meditation, and peer reflection, you can create a healthy and constructive reflection practice.

This journey toward mindful reflection can be transformative, allowing you not only to learn from your experiences but also to foster a deeper connection to the game. As you cultivate a non-judgmental approach to your reflections, you empower yourself to embrace challenges, celebrate achievements, and nurture your growth as a golfer.

By remaining curious and open during your reflective process, you will discover that every round, regardless of the outcome, offers valuable lessons that contribute to your overall development. Embrace the art of reflection, and let it enhance your enjoyment of the game as you continue to grow, learn, and thrive on your golfing journey.

6.2: Learning from Mistakes and Celebrating Successes Mindfully

Golf is a game that is inherently rich with both challenges and triumphs. Each round presents a unique opportunity to learn from mistakes while simultaneously offering moments to celebrate successes. However, the way we process these experiences profoundly influences our growth and enjoyment of the sport. Understanding the balance between reflection on our errors and acknowledgment of our achievements is key to becoming a well-rounded golfer.

In this chapter, we will explore the critical importance of learning from mistakes and celebrating successes through a mindful lens. Mindfulness allows us to embrace both aspects of our game—perceiving challenges not as obstacles but as valuable lessons, and recognising victories, regardless of their size, as affirmations of our dedication and effort. This mindful approach encourages golfers to view their experiences holistically, fostering personal development and deeper fulfilment in their golfing journey.

By adopting strategies that promote mindful reflection on mistakes, players can cultivate resilience, enabling them to bounce back from setbacks and transform them into opportunities for learning and improvement. Equally important is the practice of celebrating successes, which nurtures a positive mind-set and reinforces a sense of achievement. This dual focus helps to solidify one's confidence on the course, creating a foundation for future growth.

As we delve into the techniques for effectively processing both mistakes and successes mindfully, you will discover how this balance enhances not only your performance but also your connection to the sport. By embracing this journey of continuous learning and appreciation, you can transform each round of golf into a meaningful experience—one rich with insights, enjoyment, and a profound sense of purpose. Join us as we explore how the mindful practice of reflecting on your experiences can lead to outstanding personal growth and a lifelong love for the game of golf.

The Role of Mistakes in Golf

Mistakes are an inevitable part of the golfing journey, and how we respond to these missteps can significantly shape our overall perception of the sport. While mistakes often induce feelings of frustration and self-doubt, they also provide invaluable lessons that can enhance both resilience and skill. By reframing mistakes as opportunities for learning and personal growth, golfers can transform their approach to the game, fostering a healthier mind-set and a deeper connection to their craft.

Identifying areas for improvement is one of the key benefits of recognising mistakes. Each misjudged shot, inconsistent swing, or lapse in course management serves as a valuable indicator of aspects that require attention. For instance, a wayward drive may signal the need to focus on alignment, while a missed putt might highlight areas where additional practice is needed. Each mistake presents a chance to assess your performance critically and identify specific skills to address in your practice sessions.

Furthermore, embracing mistakes fosters a growth mind-set—an essential attitude in golf that promotes resilience. By viewing challenges as opportunities for improvement rather than as failures, golfers can approach their game with a sense of curiosity and determination. This shift in perspective not only alleviates the pressure associated with competition but also nurtures a more positive relationship with the sport. As players learn to accept that mistakes are simply part of the learning process, they bolster their emotional resilience, allowing them to weather the inevitable ups and downs of the game.

Mistakes also encourage reflection and adjustment. When golfers acknowledge their errors, they unlock the door to meaningful reflection, which is crucial for understanding what went wrong and how to adjust their approaches in future rounds. This reflective practice allows for a deeper exploration of both mental and physical components of their game, ensuring that valuable insights inform future performance. By committing to this process of reflection, golfers can turn past shortcomings into critical learning experiences that ultimately elevate their game.

In summary, the role of mistakes in golf is not to be feared but embraced. They provide essential opportunities for growth, self-discovery, and improved performance. By recognising mistakes as stepping stones along your golfing journey and adopting a compassionate and reflective approach, you can transform challenges into valuable lessons. As you navigate the intricacies of the game, remember that each error is a chance to learn, adapt, and ultimately thrive on and off the course.

Mindful Techniques for Learning from Mistakes

To effectively process mistakes mindfully and foster a constructive learning experience, golfers can implement a variety of techniques that encourage self-reflection and growth. By embracing these practices, individuals can transform errors into valuable lessons that enhance their overall performance and enjoyment of the game.

1. **Accept and Acknowledge Your Mistakes:** Acceptance is the crucial first step in the journey toward transforming mistakes into learning opportunities. By acknowledging what went wrong without casting judgment, you create a safe space for valuable learning to occur. This mindful acceptance is vital for maintaining a healthy perspective on your golfing experience.

Technique:

1. After completing your round, carve out some quiet time to reflect on your errors. Take your journal and objectively write down what happened during the round, noting the specific mistakes and how they affected your game. This clarity helps to solidify your understanding of your performance.
2. It is essential to avoid labelling your mistakes as failures. Rather than viewing them through a critical lens, recognise these missteps simply as experiences from which you can learn and grow. This shift in perspective empowers you to engage with your challenges constructively.
3. Allow yourself to feel any emotions associated with these mistakes—whether it be frustration, disappointment, or annoyance—but do not dwell on them. Acknowledge these feelings as they arise, and permit them to pass through your awareness without lingering. Recognising and accepting your emotional responses fosters resilience and emotional awareness.

Practicing acceptance facilitates a healthier response to mistakes. By detaching from negative emotions and focusing instead on constructive analysis, you open the door to meaningful insights that can inform your future practice and play. This mindful engagement with your errors encourages a growth mind-set, allowing you to approach each challenge with curiosity and determination. Embracing this technique not only enhances your reflective practice but also deepens your connection to the game, transforming the way you learn from your experiences on the course. By cultivating the capacity to accept and acknowledge your mistakes, you empower yourself to foster resilience, adaptability, and a profound appreciation for the journey of growth that golf represents.

2. **Analyse the Situation Constructively:** After acknowledging your mistakes, the next crucial step is to analyse them constructively. Understanding the factors that contributed to an error can illuminate a pathway forward, guiding your growth as a golfer and informing your future practice.

Technique:

1. **Performance Review:** Begin by reviewing your performance holistically, focusing on the specific circumstances surrounding each mistake. Consider key factors such as your mental state, physical execution, and the environmental conditions that may have influenced your shots. This reflective analysis provides context and helps you identify patterns in your performance.
2. **Ask Targeted Questions:** Engage in introspective questioning to deepen your understanding of your experiences. Ask yourself questions like, "What was I thinking at that moment?" or "What could I have done differently?" This inquiry encourages critical thinking and self-awareness, enabling you to dissect your performance with clarity.
3. **Develop Actionable Strategies:** Based on your analysis and reflections, identify one or two actionable strategies for improvement. This could involve adjusting your practice focus to target specific weaknesses, refining your mental approach for upcoming rounds, or seeking feedback from trusted peers or coaches. Establishing these strategies ensures that you consistently move forward, using past experiences to guide your development.

Engaging in constructive analysis empowers you to actively learn from your mistakes, transforming negative experiences into valuable opportunities for growth. By adopting this mind-set, you can enhance your resilience, allowing for a more adaptive and positive approach to both golf and daily challenges. Recognising that mistakes are not final destinations but stepping stones along the journey fosters a deeper appreciation for the learning process, ultimately contributing to your evolution as a golfer.

3. **Practice Self-Compassion in Reflection**: In addition to analysing your mistakes, practicing self-compassion during the reflection process is vital for maintaining motivation and a positive mind-set. Self-compassion involves treating yourself with kindness and understanding, allowing you to embrace your experiences fully without harsh judgment.

Technique:

1. **Cultivate Kindness**: As you engage in reflection, make a conscious effort to speak kindly to yourself. Remind yourself that every golfer makes mistakes, and that learning is an integral part of the journey. Embracing this gentle self-talk fosters a supportive internal environment that encourages growth.
2. **Reframe Your Inner Dialogue**: Transform your self-criticism into encouragement. For instance, instead of berating yourself with thoughts like, "I can't believe I missed that putt," reframe it to something more constructive, such as, "I can learn from this experience and do better next time." This shift in perspective empowers you to view challenges not as failures but as essential components of your development.
3. **Write a Self-Compassionate Letter**: Consider writing a letter to yourself that focuses on what you've learned from your mistakes. Acknowledge your commitment to growth and the progress you've made, regardless of the setbacks. This written reflection serves as a tangible reminder of your journey and reinforces your dedication to self-improvement.

Practicing self-compassion fosters emotional resilience, enabling you to approach future challenges with a constructive mind-set. By granting yourself the kindness and understanding that you would offer a friend, you create a safe space for growth and learning. This nurturing practice encourages you to embrace the full spectrum of your experiences—both the triumphs and the trials—ultimately enhancing your overall well-being and performance on the course.

In summary, by integrating the techniques of constructive analysis and self-compassion into your reflection routine, you can cultivate a more enriching and positive approach to your golfing journey. These practices not only support your development as a player but also promote a deeper connection to the sport, allowing you to enjoy the growth process and the game itself. Embrace this journey of mindful reflection, and discover the profound impact it can have on your performance and personal fulfilment.

The Significance of Celebrating Successes

Equally important as learning from mistakes is the practice of celebrating your successes. Acknowledging and embracing achievements—regardless of their size—reinforces positive experiences and serves as a powerful motivator for continued growth. In the realm of golf, where both triumphs and challenges abound, recognising your successes can foster a healthier mind-set and deepen your connection to the game.

First and foremost, celebrating successes **builds confidence**. Each time you acknowledge a positive experience, whether it be a well-executed shot, a strategic decision, or simply maintaining composure under pressure, you strengthen your self-belief on the course. This boost in confidence allows you to play with greater assurance, transforming your mental landscape into one of possibility rather than doubt.

Furthermore, recognising what worked well in your game plays a crucial role in **reinforcing positive behaviour**. When you identify and celebrate successful behaviours and strategies, you create a roadmap for future rounds. This awareness enables you to replicate those effective techniques, contributing to greater consistency and improved performance in subsequent games. Each success becomes a stepping stone, guiding you towards achieving your golfing goals.

Celebrating milestones also contributes to **creating joy and connection** within the golfing community. Sharing your accomplishments with fellow golfers fosters a sense of camaraderie, as you collectively celebrate the highs of the game. These shared moments not only deepen your appreciation for the sport but also strengthen the bonds with your golfing partners. Acknowledging each other's successes creates an uplifting atmosphere that enhances the overall experience of playing together.

In summary, the significance of celebrating successes cannot be overstated. By consciously recognising your achievements, you not only build confidence and reinforce positive behaviours but also cultivate joy and connection within the golfing community. Embrace the practice of celebrating successes as an essential component of your journey, and allow it to inspire you towards greater heights in your game. The moments of triumph, no matter how small, are what enrich your experience as a golfer, transforming each round into an opportunity for personal growth and joyful connection.

Mindful Techniques for Celebrating Successes

Incorporating mindfulness into your celebrations can significantly amplify their positive effects, enriching the experience of acknowledging achievements both personally and within the golfing community. This chapter outlines effective techniques to celebrate successes mindfully, allowing you to deepen your appreciation for your journey and foster connections with others.

1. **Reflect on Your Achievements:** Taking time to reflect on your successes after each round is essential, regardless of whether it's a par made, a challenging shot executed well, or simply a day spent enjoying the game. Mindful reflection allows you to fully appreciate your accomplishments and the effort you put forth.

Technique:

> Begin by finding a quiet space to sit after your round. Close your eyes and take a few deep breaths, allowing your mind to settle and your body to relax. As you breathe, draw forth specific moments of success from the day's play. These may include successful shots, strategic decisions that paid off, or instances where you maintained composure under pressure.
>
> Visualise these achievements as vividly as possible; immerse yourself in the sensations of those moments. Focus not only on the actions themselves but also on the emotions they evoked—feelings of pride, excitement, or relief. Take a few moments to genuinely appreciate your efforts and the things you did well throughout the round. To solidify these positive reflections, consider writing them down in a journal. This act of documentation reinforces the moments of joy and accomplishment in your mind.
>
> Reflecting mindfully on your successes reinforces positive emotions and strengthens your motivation to continue striving for improvement. By anchoring yourself in these uplifting experiences, you cultivate a mind-set filled with gratitude and optimism that fuels your future endeavours.

2. **Share Your Successes with Others:** Sharing your achievements with fellow golfers or friends can greatly enhance the joy derived from those successes. Celebrating together fosters a sense of community, support, and mutual encouragement that enriches the overall experience of playing golf.

Technique:

After your round, engage in meaningful conversations with your golfing partners about the highlights of the day. Take turns sharing your specific successes while also inquiring about their experiences, thereby creating an atmosphere of camaraderie and shared joy.

Consider utilising social media or golfing forums to announce your accomplishments, whether it's a new personal best, a particularly great shot, or simply the satisfaction of a well-played game. Celebrating these positive experiences with your broader golfing community helps reinforce connections and positivity.

Additionally, organise friendly get-togethers with fellow golfers to celebrate not just individual wins, but also the collective accomplishments of your group. This shared celebration can take the form of informal gatherings or friendly competitions, underscoring the importance of community and shared enjoyment in the sport.

Sharing your successes magnifies their positive effects, allowing you and your fellow golfers to revel in joy together. Establishing a supportive environment fosters ongoing growth and motivation, as each player encourages and uplifts the others, enriching the sense of belonging within the golfing community.

3. **Create Personal Milestones:** Setting personal milestones and achievement indicators is an effective strategy for actively celebrating progress throughout your golfing journey. These objectives enable you to measure your development more effectively while promoting essential self-acknowledgment of your efforts and achievements.

Technique:

To begin, take the time at the start of each golf season to set specific and measurable goals for your game. Consider what skills you want to improve, the target scores you aspire to achieve, and how many days per week you wish to dedicate to practice. These clear goals provide a roadmap for your practice sessions, keeping you focused on your desired outcomes.

Once you have established your overarching goals, it's important to break them down into smaller, incremental milestones. For example, if your aim is to enhance your short game, create specific milestones for each element, such as chipping, putting, or pitching. This step-by-step approach not only makes your goals more manageable but also offers opportunities to celebrate achievements along the way.

As you reach each milestone, take the time to celebrate and acknowledge your hard work. This could be expressed through ritualistic gestures, such as reflecting on your journey, sharing your achievement with friends, or treating yourself to a small reward. Celebrating these moments fosters motivation and reinforces the belief in your capacity to improve and succeed.

Creating personal milestones fosters a strong sense of purpose and motivation, encouraging you to maintain focus on your growth while simultaneously celebrating each accomplishment, no matter how small. This practice cultivates a positive mind-set, reminding you that each step forward is a victory in itself and reinforcing your engagement with the game of golf.

4. **Practice Gratitude:** Developing a gratitude practice related to your golfing journey can profoundly enhance your overall mind-set, enabling you to appreciate the rich tapestry of experiences, connections, and learning opportunities that the game provides. Gratitude serves as a powerful tool for fostering a sense of fulfilment and joy within your golfing experience.

Technique:

At the end of each round, take a moment to reflect on at least three things you are grateful for regarding your experience that day. These can range from the natural beauty of the surroundings to specific interactions with fellow golfers or even the lessons learned from challenging situations. This simple act of reflection encourages positivity and a mind-set rooted in appreciation.

Consider keeping a dedicated gratitude journal for your golf experiences, where you can jot down the lessons learned, memorable moments, and instances that brought you joy. This journal serves as a tangible reminder of the good times and personal growth you encounter as you navigate the sport.

Additionally, share your expressions of gratitude with your fellow golfers. This practice can spark meaningful conversations about positive experiences and reinforce a sense of community centred on appreciation. By openly discussing what you are thankful for, you create an environment that nurtures mutual support and encouragement.

Practicing gratitude promotes a positive mind-set, allowing you to cherish both your successes and learning experiences while fostering a deeper love for the game. As you cultivate this practice, you will find that it enriches your connection to golf, enabling you to approach each round with an open heart and a renewed sense of appreciation. Embracing gratitude not only enhances your experience on the course but also carries the potential to transform your overall outlook on life, inviting joy and satisfaction into every aspect of your golfing journey.

Conclusion

By consciously practicing mindful techniques for celebrating successes, you enhance not only your personal experience but also contribute to a nurturing golfing culture. Embracing reflection and sharing as integral components of your journey allows you to transform your approach to the game, deepening your appreciation for every round played. As you celebrate not just your victories but also those of your peers, you create an uplifting atmosphere that encourages shared learning and fosters lasting connections within the golfing community.

The processes of learning from mistakes and celebrating successes go hand in hand in fostering growth as a golfer. By employing techniques such as acceptance, constructive analysis, self-compassion, achievement sharing, personal milestones, and gratitude, you can cultivate a balanced approach to reflection. This strategy enables you to navigate the intricacies of your golfing journey, recognising that both successes and challenges are pivotal to your development as a player.

Embracing mistakes as valuable learning opportunities while celebrating your accomplishments reinforces positive behaviours, builds confidence, and nurtures resilience. This holistic approach to reflection not only enhances your skills on the course but also enriches your relationship with the sport, allowing you to find joy and fulfilment in every outing.

As you continue your golfing journey, remember that each experience—whether it be a challenge or a victory—is a stepping stone toward becoming the golfer you aspire to be. Embrace these moments with an open heart and a reflective mind, letting your passion for the sport guide you forward on the path to continual growth and discovery.

Chapter 7: Mindfulness Off the Course

While golf is undoubtedly a sport that demands focus and precision, the principles of mindfulness extend far beyond the fairways and greens. The skills and practices developed through mindfulness on the course can be seamlessly integrated into everyday life, offering a holistic approach to well-being that enhances both personal and professional aspects of our existence. This chapter highlights the importance of applying mindfulness off the course and explores how it can enrich our relationships, manage stress, and improve overall quality of life.

Incorporating mindfulness into daily activities encourages us to cultivate awareness and presence in every moment. Whether it's engaging in meaningful conversations, navigating the challenges of work, or simply finding joy in the ordinary tasks of life, the practice of mindfulness allows us to approach our experiences with clarity and intention. By fostering a mindful mind-set off the course, we can develop resilience, emotional regulation, and a greater appreciation for the world around us.

Throughout this chapter, we will delve into various mindful practices that can easily fit into your daily routine. From mindful communication and stress management techniques to practices that enhance self-care and overall satisfaction, these strategies are designed to help you live more intentionally and cultivate a deeper connection to yourself and others.

As you explore mindfulness beyond the golf course, you'll discover that the benefits go hand in hand with your performance and enjoyment on the course. The lessons of being present, engaged, and aware can transform not only your game but also your life, enriching your understanding of who you are and how you relate to the world around you. Let's embark on this journey of integrating mindfulness into your daily life, unlocking the potential to thrive both in and out of the golfing arena.

7.1: Incorporating Mindfulness into Daily Life for Overall Well-Being

Mindfulness transcends the boundaries of the golf course; it is a profound way of living that invites individuals to cultivate awareness and presence in every moment of life. By consciously integrating mindfulness into daily routines, golfers can significantly enhance their overall well-being, foster personal growth, and enrich their enjoyment of life, both within the sport and beyond.

This chapter delves into practical strategies for weaving mindfulness into everyday activities, providing actionable insights that can lead to a more fulfilling approach to life. Whether you are at work, engaging with family and friends, or simply navigating routine tasks, these techniques empower you to deepen your connection to yourself, others, and the world around you.

By embracing mindfulness in daily life, golfers not only improve their performance on the course but also cultivate a more balanced and vibrant existence. This holistic approach encourages you to savour the small joys of life—transforming mundane moments into opportunities for reflection and appreciation. Join us as we explore how incorporating mindfulness into your everyday experiences can enhance your quality of life, foster resilience, and ultimately contribute to a more joyful and engaged way of living.

The Importance of Mindfulness in Daily Life

Embracing a mind-set of mindfulness in daily life brings forth a multitude of benefits that significantly contribute to overall well-being. One of the most immediate advantages is **reduced stress**. Mindfulness practices promote relaxation and encourage individuals to focus on the present moment, effectively diverting attention away from anxieties about the future or regrets about the past. This shift allows for a calmer mental state, reducing the impact of stressors that often accompany daily life.

Additionally, mindfulness enhances **emotional regulation** by fostering a greater awareness of one's emotions as they arise. This heightened awareness enables individuals to respond thoughtfully rather than reacting impulsively. Improved emotional intelligence, cultivated through mindful practices, can lead to stronger relationships and more effective communication, allowing for deeper connections with others.

Moreover, regularly practicing mindfulness sharpens one's ability to **focus and concentrate**. This enhanced attention can significantly improve productivity and performance in various aspects of life, from professional endeavours to personal pursuits. By training the mind to remain present, individuals become more adept at managing tasks with clarity and efficiency.

With the unpredictable nature of life, mindfulness also plays a crucial role in developing **greater resilience**. It equips individuals to cope with challenges and uncertainties, helping them adapt to changing circumstances and bounce back from setbacks. This resilience fosters a sense of empowerment, encouraging a proactive approach to problem-solving and personal growth.

Furthermore, mindfulness cultivates a deeper **appreciation for life**. By encouraging individuals to slow down and savour the simple joys—whether it's a warm cup of coffee, the beauty of nature, or meaningful moments spent with loved ones—mindfulness nurtures gratitude. This increased sense of appreciation contributes to greater overall satisfaction and happiness, enriching the fabric of daily living.

In conclusion, integrating mindfulness into your daily life paves the way for a healthier and more fulfilling existence. From reducing stress and improving emotional regulation to enhancing focus and resilience, mindfulness offers practical tools for navigating the complexities of life with grace and awareness. As you embrace these practices, you will discover that the benefits extend far beyond the golf course, providing you with a deeper sense of connection and contentment in every aspect of your life.

Practical Strategies for Incorporating Mindfulness

To enhance well-being and create a more fulfilling existence, the following strategies provide practical ways to seamlessly weave mindfulness into your everyday life. Each approach fosters a greater sense of presence and intention, ultimately enriching your experience at home, at work, and on the golf course.

1. **Mindful Mornings:** Starting each day with mindfulness is a powerful way to set a positive tone for what lies ahead. A mindful morning routine prepares you to approach the day with intention and focus, laying the groundwork for a successful and harmonious experience.

Technique:

1. Upon waking, dedicate a few moments to practicing mindful breathing. Close your eyes and notice your breath as you take deep, intentional inhales and exhales. Allow your body to gradually awaken as you immerse yourself in this calming practice.
2. Take a moment to express gratitude for the day ahead. Reflect on three things you are looking forward to or appreciate about your life in this moment. This act of gratitude cultivates a positive mind-set, enabling you to start the day on an uplifting note.

3. Engage in a few gentle stretches or yoga poses, inviting mindfulness into your physical movements. As you stretch, pay attention to the sensations in your body, fostering a connection between mind and body that enhances your awareness of physical presence.
4. Finally, set a clear intention for your day. Identify a quality you wish to embody—such as patience, focus, or gratitude—and commit to carrying this intention with you throughout your activities. By grounding your day in this purposeful mind-set, you enhance your ability to navigate challenges that may arise.

A mindful morning routine establishes a calm and intentional framework for your day. By integrating breathing exercises, gratitude, and movement, you cultivate the mental clarity and emotional resilience needed to meet daily challenges with confidence and purpose. This practice not only prepares you for the day ahead but also enriches your overall experience by fostering a deeper connection to yourself, others, and the world around you. Embrace the potential of mindful mornings, and watch as they transform the way you engage with each day.

2. **Mindful Eating:** Mindful eating is a transformative practice that emphasises savouring each bite and being fully present during meals. By engaging with food in a conscious manner, this technique encourages a healthy relationship with what you eat, enhancing both the enjoyment and nutritional benefits of your meals. Mindful eating not only fosters appreciation for the flavours and textures of food but also promotes better digestion and overall well-being.

Technique:

To begin your mindful eating practice, start each meal by taking a few deep breaths to centre your mind. This moment of pausing allows you to disconnect from the distractions of the day. Set aside your phones, turn off the television, and create a space free from interruptions, ensuring you are fully present for the meal.

Next, take a moment to appreciate the colourful array of your meal. Observe the textures, and inhale the delicious aromas that waft toward you. Engaging your senses deeply enriches the experience of eating, transforming it into a joyful ritual rather than a hurried obligation.

As you begin to eat, do so slowly and deliberately. Chew each bite thoroughly, taking time to notice the flavours and sensations as they unfold in your mouth. This practice not only enhances your enjoyment of the meal but also allows you to become more attuned to the experience of eating, ultimately nurturing a sense of gratitude for the nourishment you receive.

Throughout your meal, listen closely to your body's hunger cues and respond with kindness. Pay attention to how your body feels as you eat, recognising when you are satisfied or full. This heightened awareness helps you cultivate a compassionate approach to eating, encouraging healthier habits that align with your body's needs.

The benefits of mindful eating are profound. By fostering a deeper connection with food, this practice allows individuals to cultivate awareness of their nutritional choices, leading to healthier eating habits and improved overall well-being. As you embrace mindful eating, you'll find that meals become opportunities for reflection and nourishment, enriching both your physical health and emotional satisfaction.

Ultimately, mindful eating transforms the act of dining into a holistic experience. By fully engaging with your food, you create a pathway toward healthier lifestyle choices, fostering a sense of balance and harmony within yourself. Embrace this practice, and watch as it enhances not only your relationship with food but also your overall approach to wellness and satisfaction in life.

3. **Incorporating Mindfulness into Physical Activity:** Incorporating mindfulness into your physical activities—whether you're engaging in a rigorous workout, practicing yoga, or simply going for a leisurely walk—can immensely enhance both your physical and mental state. By infusing mindfulness into these movements, you not only elevate the quality of the activity but also cultivate a deeper connection with your body, fostering a greater sense of well-being.

Technique:

1. **Tune Into Your Body**: As you engage in physical activity, start by focusing on the sensations within your body. Pay attention to the rhythm of your breath, the movement of your muscles, and the connection of your feet with the ground. This heightened awareness allows you to experience each moment fully, enhancing your enjoyment and understanding of your physical capabilities.

2. **Utilise Visualisation Techniques**: Enhance your movements by employing visualisation techniques. For instance, as you exercise, vividly picture the strength and fluidity of each motion. Visualising these aspects can amplify your focus and reinforce a sense of empowerment, motivating you to push through your limits while maintaining proper form.
3. **Practice Gratitude**: Cultivating a sense of gratitude for your body's ability to move is an essential element of mindful physical activity. Acknowledge the effort you're investing in your physical health, appreciating how your body functions and supports you in every endeavour. This appreciation fosters a positive relationship with your body and encourages you to treat it with respect and kindness.
4. **Maintain Present-Moment Awareness**: As you engage in your chosen activity, strive to stay present in the moment. If your mind begins to wander—whether to worries, future tasks, or past experiences—gently redirect your focus back to your breathing and the physical sensations you are experiencing. This practice of returning to the present strengthens your mindfulness and contributes to greater emotional resilience.

Mindful physical activity allows you to appreciate each movement and develop a more positive relationship with your body. This enriching practice not only improves your physical fitness but also enhances your mental health, fostering emotional clarity and resilience. By fully engaging with each exercise, you create an opportunity for self-discovery and holistic health that extends beyond just physical performance.

When mindfulness becomes an integral part of your physical activity, you cultivate an enriched understanding of your body's capabilities and establish a deeper connection with the joy of movement. Embracing this practice empowers you to approach fitness and well-being with intention, transforming every session into a fulfilling experience that nourishes both body and mind. As you integrate mindfulness into your physical activities, you'll discover a pathway to improved health, well-being, and overall satisfaction in your daily life.

4. **Mindful Communication:** Mindful communication is an essential practice that fosters deeper connections with others while enhancing understanding and empathy in every interaction. In a world filled with distractions and fast-paced conversations, embracing mindfulness in our communication can lead to more meaningful exchanges and enriched relationships.

Technique:

1. **Give Full Attention**: During conversations, commit to giving your full attention to the speaker. This means practicing active listening, which involves making eye contact and using nods or other nonverbal cues to demonstrate your engagement and understanding. By being fully present, you convey to the speaker that their words and feelings matter.
2. **Practice Presence**: Avoid the urge to interrupt or start planning your response while the other person is speaking. Instead, focus on their words and the emotions behind them. This level of attentiveness allows you to truly hear what is being said and fosters an environment of trust and openness.
3. **Respond Empathetically**: When it's your turn to express your thoughts and feelings, do so honestly and with empathy. Acknowledge the emotions of the other person by using validating phrases such as "I hear you" or "That makes sense." This approach reinforces their viewpoint and fosters a supportive dialogue, enhancing understanding and connection.
4. **Maintain Composure**: If you feel emotions rising during a conversation—whether it be frustration, excitement, or sadness—take a moment to breathe deeply before responding. This practice of pausing allows you to maintain composure and reflect thoughtfully on your words, ensuring that your response is mindful and considerate.

The practice of mindful communication fosters strong relationships by promoting mutual understanding and reducing misunderstandings. When conversations are approached with mindfulness, they become opportunities for compassion and respect, creating a supportive atmosphere that benefits all parties involved.

Moreover, engaging in mindful communication deepens emotional connections, allowing for richer interactions and a greater appreciation for the perspectives of others. As you cultivate this practice in your daily life, you will find that it enhances not only your interactions on the golf course—whether with fellow players or support staff—but also those in your personal and professional realms.

In essence, embracing mindful communication enhances your overall quality of life, encouraging a more empathetic and conscious way of engaging with the world around you. As you practice these techniques, remember that the connections you forge through mindful dialogue contribute to a more compassionate and understanding society, one conversation at a time.

5. **Mindful Moments Throughout the Day:** Incorporating small moments of mindfulness throughout your day can profoundly impact your overall well-being. These brief practices serve as powerful tools for activating present-moment awareness, effectively helping to reduce stress and enhance focus. By weaving mindfulness into the fabric of your daily activities, you nurture a deeper connection to yourself and your surroundings, ultimately cultivating a more fulfilling life.

Technique:

1. **Set Reminders for Mindfulness**: Begin by creating reminders for yourself to pause and take a deep breath throughout the day. Utilise phone alarms, app notifications, or sticky notes placed strategically around your living or workspaces. These gentle nudges will prompt you to halt the busyness of life and engage in a moment of mindfulness.
2. **Pause and Breathe**: When you receive these reminders, take a moment to close your eyes and focus on your breath. Inhale deeply through your nose, allowing your abdomen to expand fully, and then exhale slowly through your mouth. This brief pause not only helps reset your mind and body but also fosters a sense of clarity as you re-centre your thoughts.
3. **Mindfulness in Everyday Activities**: Engage in simple, everyday activities with a mindful approach. Whether washing dishes, taking a shower, or brushing your teeth, immerse yourself in the sensations and movements involved in the task. Notice the feel of the water, the texture of the soap, or the rhythm of your actions as you engage fully with these experiences.
4. **Acknowledge and Refocus**: When transitioning from one task to another, take a moment to notice how your body feels and what thoughts arise. Observe these sensations and thoughts without judgment, allowing them to exist in your awareness. After acknowledging them, gently redirect your focus back to your next activity, cultivating a continuous connection to the present.

By forming a habit of embedding mindful moments throughout your day, you cultivate a greater sense of presence and calmness. These practices encourage you to navigate daily challenges with clarity and ease, reducing the overwhelming feelings that can accumulate in our fast-paced lives.

Ultimately, the incorporation of mindful moments fosters increased emotional resilience and well-being. As you embrace these brief yet impactful practices, you will find that they help you maintain a balanced perspective, enriching both your personal and professional experiences. Mindfulness transforms moments of routine into opportunities for reflection and engagement, enabling you to live each day with greater awareness and appreciation. By embracing the art of mindfulness, you can create a more harmonious and satisfying existence, both on and off the golf course.

6. **Mindful Reflection Before Sleep:** Ending your day with mindfulness is an invaluable practice that promotes relaxation and prepares your mind for restful sleep, while also solidifying the lessons and experiences gleaned from your day. By dedicating time each evening to engage in mindful reflection, you create a peaceful transition from the busyness of daily life to the serene state necessary for restorative rest.

Technique:

1. **Set Aside Time for Reflection**: Before bed, allocate a few quiet moments to engage in mindful reflection. Choose a tranquil space where you can sit comfortably or lie down without distractions. This dedicated time gently signals to your mind and body that it is time to unwind and reflect.
2. **Begin with Deep Breaths**: Start your mindful session with a few deep breaths, allowing your body to relax and gradually slow down. Inhale deeply through your nose, filling your lungs, and then exhale slowly through your mouth. As you breathe, take note of any areas of tension in your body and consciously release them, letting go of the day's stress and strain.
3. **Reflect Without Judgment**: As you settle into a state of relaxation, begin to reflect on your day gently. Allow yourself to contemplate what went well, the moments of connection you experienced, and the challenges you faced without assigning judgment to those reflections. Focus on the learning opportunities that each experience provided, recognising growth as a natural part of your journey.
4. **Cultivate Gratitude**: To enhance your reflection, practice gratitude by consciously acknowledging three things you are thankful for that day, no matter how small. This could be a compliment from a fellow golfer, a beautiful moment spent in nature, or simply the satisfaction of striving to be your best.

> Expressing gratitude before sleep helps cultivate a positive mindset, creating a nurturing environment for rest.

Engaging in mindful reflection at night yields a multitude of benefits. This practice promotes emotional release and clarity, facilitating a peaceful state of mind that allows you to sleep more soundly. By processing the events of the day with a compassionate lens, you free yourself from lingering worries and stressors, paving the way for restorative sleep.

Moreover, this mindful approach prepares you to wake up rejuvenated and ready to embrace the challenges of a new day. By cultivating a habit of nightly reflection, you not only enhance your emotional well-being but also establish a deeper understanding of yourself and your experiences. As you continue to incorporate this practice into your evening routine, you'll find that it enriches both your personal growth and your enjoyment of the journey ahead—on and off the golf course. Embrace the art of mindful reflection as an integral part of your life, and allow it to transform your evenings into a sanctuary of peace and gratitude.

Conclusion

Incorporating mindfulness into daily life is a powerful practice that enhances overall well-being and personal fulfilment. By engaging in mindful mornings, conscious eating, physical activity, communication, and reflection, you cultivate a deeper connection to yourself and those around you.

This holistic approach to mindfulness not only enriches your golf game but also positively impacts your relationships, decision-making, and emotional resilience. Each mindful moment, no matter how small, nourishes your mental state and nurtures a greater appreciation for life's experiences.

As you embark on this journey of mindfulness, remember that it is not about achieving perfection but rather about engaging fully with each moment. Embrace the process of being present, allowing it to enhance your life on and off the course. With consistent practice, mindfulness can transform everyday activities into opportunities for growth, joy, and deeper connection, leading to a more fulfilling, balanced life. Remember, the journey of mindfulness is a lifelong commitment—each day offers a new chance to practice presence and cultivate well-being.

7.2: Building a Lifestyle That Supports Mental and Physical Health

The intricate relationship between mental and physical health is profoundly impactful, especially for athletes. In the game of golf, where both the mind and body play critical roles, establishing a lifestyle that nurtures overall well-being is essential for maximising performance and enhancing enjoyment of the sport. This chapter delves into effective strategies for creating a balanced lifestyle that supports both mental and physical health, ultimately fostering resilience and enriching the overall golfing experience.

As golfers navigate the complexities of their sport, it becomes clear that success hinges not only on physical prowess but also on the mental fortitude cultivated through healthy habits. A holistic approach to well-being encompasses various components, including nutrition, physical fitness, mental practices, and social connections. By integrating these elements into their daily routines, golfers can create a lifestyle that enhances their performance and nurtures their love for the game.

In this chapter, we will explore actionable strategies that you can implement to cultivate a lifestyle supportive of mental and physical health. From committing to regular physical activity and maintaining a balanced diet to incorporating mindfulness practices and fostering social connections, each element contributes to a foundation of resilience and vitality. By embracing these components, you empower yourself not only to excel in your golf game but also to thrive in all areas of life.

Moreover, the benefits of establishing such a lifestyle extend beyond the game itself. By prioritising mental and physical well-being, golfers cultivate a deeper sense of joy and fulfilment, enriching their overall golfing journey. With a focus on balance and harmony between mind and body, you will be better equipped to navigate the challenges of both sport and life, approaching each day with renewed energy, clarity, and a passion for growth.

As we embark on this exploration of lifestyle strategies, prepare to discover how integrating mindfulness and health-conscious practices can lead to remarkable transformations both on and off the golf course. Embrace the journey toward a lifestyle that supports your mental and physical health, and experience the profound impact it can have on your performance, well-being, and enjoyment of the beautiful game of golf.

The Connection Between Mental and Physical Health

The intricate link between mental and physical health is both profound and essential, particularly in the realm of sports. For golfers, understanding how these two facets of well-being influence one another is crucial for optimising both performance on the course and overall quality of life. Poor mental health can undermine physical performance, just as physical ailments can lead to mental strain. Recognising this relationship is key to fostering a lifestyle that enhances both game and well-being.

The benefits of adopting a lifestyle that integrates mental and physical health are manifold. First and foremost, **enhanced performance** is a significant advantage. A healthy body supports a clear and focused mind, enabling golfers to concentrate more effectively, react swiftly to changing situations, and execute shots with enhanced precision. This harmonious interplay between mind and body contributes to more consistent and successful outcomes on the course.

Additionally, adopting a holistic approach to well-being leads to **increased resilience**. Building both mental and physical strength empowers golfers to cope with the inherent challenges of competition and effectively navigate setbacks. This resilience is critical not only for maintaining performance during high-stakes moments but also for fostering a positive attitude and determination in the face of adversity.

An integrated lifestyle also translates to **improved well-being** beyond the confines of the golf course. Regular physical activity paired with mindfulness practices enhances emotional regulation and reduces anxiety, cultivating a sense of balance and peace. This holistic approach fosters an improved overall quality of life, allowing golfers to experience greater contentment both in their sport and daily life.

Lastly, maintaining a balanced lifestyle results in **sustained enjoyment** of the game. A foundation of energy and vitality enhances the joy of playing golf, encouraging consistent participation and engagement with the sport. This enduring enthusiasm not only supports individual growth and development but also nurtures a deeper appreciation for the game itself.

By embracing a lifestyle that integrates mental and physical health, golfers unlock the potential to achieve remarkable performance and fulfil their aspirations. This holistic approach nurtures resilience, promotes well-being, and enriches the overall experience of playing golf, creating a path for long-term success and enjoyment. As you embark on this journey toward balance and harmony, remember that the pursuit of integrated health is a continuous process that offers rewards not just in your game, but in every aspect of your life.

Strategies for Building a Supportive Lifestyle

Creating a lifestyle that nurtures both mental and physical health is foundational for sustained well-being and optimal performance both on and off the golf course. The following strategies provide practical guidance to help you achieve this balance, fostering a harmonious connection between your mind and body.

1. **Regular Physical Activity:** Incorporating regular physical activity into your routine is essential for maintaining both physical fitness and mental clarity. Engaging your body in movement not only strengthens muscles and improves cardiovascular health but also enhances emotional well-being and mental focus—a critical combination for golfers seeking consistent improvement.

Technique:

Begin by exploring various activities that you genuinely enjoy. Whether it's walking through your local park, cycling along scenic trails, practicing yoga for balance and flexibility, or swimming for cardiovascular endurance, finding an exercise that brings you joy increases the likelihood of making it a consistent part of your lifestyle. The pleasure derived from these activities ensures sustained involvement and greater adherence to a fitness routine.

Aim for a balanced exercise regimen that encompasses cardiovascular workouts, strength training, and flexibility exercises. Each component supports different facets of physical health, collectively contributing to enhanced performance in golf. While cardiovascular exercises boost stamina and endurance, strength training fortifies muscles, and flexibility work, like yoga or stretching, improves range of motion—all factors that optimise your golf game.

Set realistic goals for your activity levels, and pay attention to how your body feels. As you gain strength and endurance, progressively increase the duration and intensity of your workouts. This gradual advancement prevents injury and keeps you motivated, as you witness tangible improvements in both your athletic performance and overall health.

Engaging in regular physical activity supports physical fitness and releases endorphins, the body's natural mood elevators. These endorphins not only improve mood and reduce stress but also foster an overall sense of well-being. The mental clarity and emotional balance cultivated through consistent exercise enhance your ability to remain focused, resilient, and positive as you approach life's challenges and the game of golf.

By incorporating these strategies into your daily routine, you establish a strong foundation for a lifestyle that supports both mental and physical health. This comprehensive approach not only enriches your golfing experience but also elevates your quality of life, allowing you to thrive with vitality and purpose. Embrace the art of building a supportive lifestyle and watch as it transforms your approach to golf, well-being, and personal growth.

2. **Balanced Nutrition:** Balanced nutrition plays an indispensable role in sustaining energy, enhancing focus, and supporting recovery, particularly for those engaging in the physically and mentally demanding game of golf. By adhering to a balanced and nutritious diet, you can optimise your overall physical health, ensuring that you are prepared to perform at your best both on and off the course.

Technique:

Prioritise the consumption of whole foods, such as fresh fruits, a variety of vibrant vegetables, lean proteins, whole grains, and healthy fats. These nutrient-dense foods provide the essential vitamins and minerals necessary for optimal physical performance and cognitive function. Emphasising whole foods in your diet ensures that your body receives the sustenance required for energy and clarity, enabling you to face each round with vigour and focus.

Staying hydrated is equally important—maintain your hydration by drinking plenty of water throughout the day. Proper hydration is critical for sustaining focus, physical energy, and endurance, particularly during rounds of golf or other physical activities. Hydration supports not only cardiovascular function but also the mental acuity needed to effectively strategise and execute shots on the course.

Advance planning and meal preparation can facilitate adherence to a nutritious diet by ensuring that healthy options are readily available, especially on days dedicated to golfing or other physical pursuits. By preparing meals ahead of time, you reduce the temptation to reach for less nutritious alternatives when time is limited or convenience is prioritised. This foresight helps maintain consistency in your dietary habits, supporting sustained energy and performance.

A balanced diet is instrumental in improving physical health, boosting energy levels, and enhancing cognitive function. By providing the body with high-quality nutrients, you bolster your capacity to perform at your highest level, whether on the golf course or in daily life. The nourishment derived from a balanced diet fosters vitality and resilience, empowering you to approach life and golf with enthusiasm, clarity, and determination.

Incorporating these nutritional practices into your lifestyle establishes a robust foundation for health and performance. As you prioritise balanced nutrition, you will experience the profound benefits it imparts, transforming your overall well-being and enriching your journey as a golfer. Embrace the power of mindful nourishment, and witness its transformative impact on your energy, focus, and enjoyment, both on the course and beyond.

3. **Mindfulness Practices:** Incorporating mindfulness practices into your daily routine is essential for maintaining mental health and emotional well-being. These practices serve as foundational tools that empower individuals to navigate the complexities of life with greater ease, resilience, and clarity. By making mindfulness a priority in your day-to-day activities, you can cultivate a mind-set that enhances both personal growth and performance on the golf course.

Technique:

1. **Daily Mindfulness Engagement:** Begin by integrating daily mindfulness practices such as meditation, deep breathing exercises, or yoga into your routine. These activities are designed to reduce stress and enhance emotional resilience, creating a buffer against the pressures of both competition and everyday life. Choose a practice that resonates with you, whether it's a short meditation session in the morning, a few deep breaths before bed, or a gentle yoga practice to start your day.
2. **Create Mindful Moments:** Throughout your day, intentionally carve out moments of mindfulness. For example, while waiting in line or during your commute, practice focusing on your breath or observing your surroundings with awareness. This could mean

noticing the colours and textures of your environment or tuning into the sounds around you. By engaging fully with these moments, you cultivate present-moment awareness, enriching your daily experiences.
3. **Gratitude Journaling**: Another powerful practice is gratitude journaling, which encourages you to reflect on positive experiences and cultivate an appreciative mind-set. Set aside time each day to write down three things you are grateful for, no matter how small. This practice not only enhances emotional well-being but also helps mitigate stress by redirecting your focus toward the positive aspects of your life.

The benefits of adopting mindfulness practices are profound and far-reaching. These techniques promote emotional stability, helping individuals manage their feelings more effectively while navigating life's challenges. Enhanced focus and clarity become natural by products of mindfulness, enabling golfers to remain present and engaged during their rounds.

Additionally, the cultivation of a grateful and positive mind-set fosters a greater sense of overall well-being, allowing golfers to approach both the sport and their lives with renewed enthusiasm. Ultimately, by embracing mindfulness practices as integral components of your daily routine, you empower yourself not only to improve your performance on the course but also to enrich your quality of life as a whole. Embrace the transformative power of mindfulness, and watch as it elevates your experience in golf and beyond.

4. **Adequate Rest and Recovery:** Adequate rest and recovery are as essential to a golfer's success as rigorous training. Just as athletes dedicate time to honing their physical skills, allowing both the body and mind to rejuvenate is critical for maintaining optimal mental and physical health. Prioritising recovery not only enhances performance but also significantly reduces the risk of burnout, which can undermine even the most dedicated golfers.

Technique:

1. **Prioritise Sleep**: Start by establishing a consistent sleep schedule, aiming for 7 to 9 hours of quality sleep each night. This commitment to restful sleep is vital for supporting recovery and cognitive function. Quality sleep enhances your body's ability to repair and regenerate, allowing you to tackle each day with renewed energy and focus.

2. **Schedule Recovery Days**: Make it a practice to carve out regular recovery days in your training regimen. These days should be dedicated to allowing your body and mind to rest and recover fully. Incorporate gentle practices such as stretching, foam rolling, or restorative yoga to promote physical recovery. Such activities enhance flexibility, reduce muscle tension, and rejuvenate your overall state.
3. **Listen to Your Body**: During your rounds, develop the habit of listening to your body. If you start to feel fatigued or mentally drained, give yourself permission to take breaks and practice self-compassion regarding your performance. Understanding the signals your body sends is crucial, allowing you to make adjustments that support your well-being and enhance your play.

The benefits of adequate rest and recovery extend beyond mere physical regeneration. Prioritising quality rest enhances physical recovery by allowing your muscles and joints to heal, promoting longevity in your golfing career. It sharpens mental clarity, enabling you to maintain focus and strategic thinking while navigating the course. Additionally, adequate recovery supports emotional stability, ensuring you approach the game with a balanced, resilient mind-set.

By recognising the importance of rest and recovery, you create a sustainable approach to both your training and competitive play. This holistic perspective not only contributes to improved performance on the course but also fosters a deeper appreciation for the game and your journey as a golfer. As you embrace the practice of adequate rest and recovery, you will discover the powerful connection between well-being and success, enhancing not only your game but also your overall quality of life. Prioritise rejuvenation, and watch as it transforms your performance and enjoyment of golf.

5. **Foster Social Connections:** Building and maintaining relationships with fellow golfers and individuals who share your interests is vital for enhancing your mental health and overall sense of well-being. Social connections foster a sense of community, alleviate feelings of loneliness, and create an uplifting environment that significantly contributes to a positive experience on the golf course.

Technique:

To foster these essential social connections, actively seek opportunities to engage with fellow golfers. Joining a local golf club can be one of the most effective ways to cultivate friendships and camaraderie.

Participating in group lessons or playing in tournaments also provides avenues for meeting like-minded individuals who share your passion for the sport. These interactions create a supportive network that enhances your enjoyment of golf, making each round an opportunity to connect and grow with others.

Additionally, schedule regular outings with friends or family who enjoy golf. Playing together not only fosters camaraderie but also enriches the experience with shared laughter and friendly competition. These outings can solidify bonds and create lasting memories, transforming an ordinary game into a cherished experience filled with support and connection.

Engaging in open conversations about your experiences on and off the course is another powerful way to deepening these relationships. Sharing your successes, challenges, and even fears with fellow golfers can create strong social bonds, allowing everyone involved to learn from one another's insights and perspectives. This exchange fosters an environment of empathy and understanding, reinforcing the idea that everyone's journey in golf—and life—is uniquely valuable.

The benefits of nurturing social connections are manifold. A strong sense of community not only enhances emotional health but also provides motivation and encouragement during both practice and competition. When you feel supported by those around you, facing challenges becomes significantly easier, allowing you to approach the game with greater confidence and resilience.

Moreover, the shared joys and successes experienced with others can amplify the satisfaction derived from playing golf, transforming each round into a celebration of both personal achievement and communal support. By fostering these social connections, you invest in your golf journey and overall well-being, enriching your life with meaningful relationships that enhance both your game and your enjoyment of the sport. Embrace the power of connection, and allow it to elevate your experiences on and off the golf course.

6. **Create a Mindful Workspace:** For those who balance golf with work or other obligations, creating a mindful workspace is a powerful way to enhance productivity and foster mental clarity. A well-designed environment can significantly impact your ability to focus, manage stress, and maintain the energy needed for both professional and athletic pursuits.

Technique:

To establish a mindful workspace, begin by organising your area to minimise clutter. A clean and orderly environment not only helps reduce distractions but also contributes to a sense of peace and purpose. When your workspace is tidy, it cultivates a mental clarity that allows you to engage more fully in your tasks, preventing the chaos of clutter from overwhelming your thoughts.

Next, incorporate elements that promote mindfulness and enhance the overall atmosphere of your workspace. Consider adding personal touches such as a vibrant plant, which can boost your mood and air quality, or calming artwork that inspires creativity and tranquillity. A small water fountain can introduce soothing sounds, creating a serene ambiance that encourages relaxation and focus. These elements contribute to a pleasant, inviting workspace that nurtures well-being and fosters a sense of connection to your surroundings.

Additionally, it's essential to take **mindful breaks** throughout your workday. Allow yourself to step away from your desk or workspace regularly, using these moments to rejuvenate your mind and body. Engage in simple activities like stretching, practicing deep breathing exercises, or stepping outside for a breath of fresh air. These pauses not only help clear your mind but also enhance your overall focus when you return to your tasks.

The benefits of creating a mindful workspace are profound. A thoughtfully designed environment enhances your ability to concentrate on your work, reduces stress levels, and promotes greater productivity. By creating a balanced workspace that supports your professional obligations and your passion for golf, you cultivate a harmonious lifestyle that enables you to excel in both domains.

Ultimately, a mindful workspace empowers you to approach your responsibilities with intention and presence, fostering a sense of balance that enriches your entire life. As you integrate these practices into your daily routine, you will find that the intersection of work and golf deepens your overall well-being, allowing you to thrive in every aspect of your journey. Embrace the opportunity to create a mindful workspace, and watch as it transforms your daily experience into one of clarity, focus, and fulfilment.

7. **Integrate Golf Practice into Your Lifestyle:** Integrating golf practice into your everyday life is essential for truly embracing the sport and elevating your skills. Rather than viewing practice as a sporadic activity, making it a fundamental part of your routine reinforces your commitment to continual improvement while nurturing your passion for the game. By prioritising golf practice, you cultivate an environment ripe for growth, enjoyment, and connection with both the sport and the community surrounding it.

Technique:

To establish this integrated approach, start by setting aside dedicated practice time each week. Whether it involves hitting balls at the driving range, honing your putting skills, or engaging in short game drills, consistency in practice is key. Carving out specific times for golf practice ensures that it becomes a regular part of your schedule, similar to any other important commitment in your life.

Consider involving friends or fellow golfers in your practice sessions. This collaboration not only enhances skill development but also fosters social connections that add depth and enjoyment to your experience. Practicing with others creates a supportive environment where you can share insights, motivate each other, and celebrate small victories together.

Further, use your practice time as an opportunity to engage in mindfulness. Focus on your technique while paying attention to your breath, allowing for a natural flow in your movements. Embrace the rhythm of your swings without the burden of overwhelming expectations about performance. This mindful approach encourages you to fully immerse yourself in the practice, which can ultimately lead to more profound growth and enjoyment.

Integrating regular golf practice into your lifestyle yields numerous benefits. Firstly, it enhances your skills, allowing you to develop a more consistent game through focused training. Furthermore, this dedicated practice deepens your love for the sport, transforming your perception of golf from merely a game to a cherished passion infused with purpose and joy.

Additionally, incorporating mindfulness into your practice provides valuable opportunities to connect with others while honing your skills. The friendships and networks you build within this framework enrich your overall experience and foster a sense of community among fellow golfers.

In summary, by weaving golf practice into the fabric of your everyday life, you promote a holistic approach to your involvement with the sport. This commitment fuels not only your technical excellence but also your emotional fulfilment and joy in playing golf. Embrace the process of integrating golf practice into your lifestyle, and witness how it enhances your journey as a golfer, allowing you to thrive both on and off the course.

Conclusion

Building a lifestyle that supports mental and physical health is essential for achieving balance and fulfilment, especially for golfers. By embracing regular physical activity, balanced nutrition, mindfulness practices, adequate rest and recovery, social connections, a mindful workspace, and consistent golf practice, you create an environment conducive to optimal well-being.

This holistic approach to healthy living transcends the golf course, enhancing your overall quality of life. Incorporating these elements into your daily routine not only prepares you to perform at your best but also allows you to find joy and satisfaction in the experience of golfing.

Remember that nurturing mental and physical health is a lifelong journey. Be gentle with yourself as you implement these practices; change takes time, and every small step contributes to your overall well-being. By living mindfully and prioritising health, you cultivate resilience, joy, and a deeper, more fulfilling connection to the game of golf and to life itself.

As you move forward, embrace each aspect of your lifestyle that nurtures both your body and mind. Celebrate your commitment to well-being, and let it inspire you not only on the golf course but in every endeavour you undertake.

Chapter 8: Tools and Resources

As you embark on your journey of mindfulness in golf and life, having the right tools and resources can significantly enhance your practice and support your growth. In this chapter, we will explore a variety of resources—ranging from apps and books to websites and community groups—that can help deepen your understanding of mindfulness and improve your skills both on and off the course.

Mindfulness is a skill that can be cultivated through continuous learning and practice, and the good news is that there are many resources available to assist you along the way. Whether you are a beginner seeking foundational knowledge or a seasoned practitioner looking to refine your techniques, this chapter offers valuable insights and recommendations tailored to meet your needs.

We'll start by highlighting some of the best apps designed to guide you through mindfulness exercises, enabling you to practice meditation, breathing techniques, and visualisation on the go. Next, we'll delve into insightful books that provide deeper perspectives on mindfulness, offering practical exercises and personal anecdotes to inspire your practice.

In addition to digital and literary resources, we will discuss online courses and websites that offer structured mindfulness training, allowing you to engage with expert guidance from the comfort of your home. Finally, we'll shine a light on community initiatives—such as local mindfulness groups and retreats—that provide opportunities for connection and shared learning experiences.

By utilising these tools and resources, you can cultivate a more enriching mindfulness practice that complements your golfing journey. Remember, mindfulness is not a destination but an ongoing journey of exploration and discovery. With the right support, you can navigate this path with confidence, enhancing your skills and creating a more profound sense of well-being in all areas of your life. Let's dive into the wealth of resources available to help you on this transformative journey toward mindfulness.

8.1: Recommended Apps, Books, and Resources for Further Mindfulness Training

In today's fast-paced world, the resources available for practicing mindfulness are more accessible than ever before. As individuals seek to deepen their practice, enhance their performance on the golf course, or cultivate a greater sense of well-being, a wealth of tools is at their disposal. From intuitive apps to insightful books, there are many resources designed to guide you on your mindfulness journey, making it easier than ever to integrate these practices into your daily life.

This chapter presents a curated list of recommended resources tailored to various aspects of mindfulness training. Each resource offers distinct features aimed at supporting your growth and development, whether you are a beginner eager to learn or a seasoned practitioner looking to refine your skills.

You will find an array of meditation apps that provide guided sessions, reminders, and progress tracking to help you stay engaged in your practice. Additionally, we will explore influential books that delve into the principles of mindfulness, providing both theoretical insights and practical exercises that enhance your understanding and application of the practice.

Moreover, we will include online courses and reputable websites that offer structured training in mindfulness and meditation. These platforms present an opportunity to learn from experts in the field, equipping you with the knowledge and tools necessary to navigate the complexities of mindfulness effectively.

Finally, we will discuss community initiatives, including local mindfulness groups and retreats, which can deepen your practice and connect you with like-minded individuals. Engaging with a supportive community can enhance your learning experience and provide encouragement as you explore the depths of mindfulness.

By utilising these recommended apps, books, and resources, you will be well-equipped to embark on or continue your mindfulness journey. Embrace the potential that mindfulness holds, and allow it to transform not only your golf game but also your overall approach to life. With the right tools at your disposal, you can navigate your path with greater awareness, clarity, and purpose.

Mindfulness Apps

Incorporating mindfulness into your daily routine has never been easier, thanks to technology. Mindfulness apps provide a convenient and accessible means of practicing mindfulness wherever you are, making it simple to integrate these transformative techniques into your life. These applications offer varied features that cater to different needs, whether you're a novice exploring the world of mindfulness or a seasoned practitioner seeking to deepen your practice. Below, we highlight some of the most popular and effective mindfulness apps available today, each designed to support and enhance your journey toward greater awareness and well-being.

1. **Headspace:** Headspace is a renowned mindfulness app that provides users with an extensive array of resources tailored to enhance both meditation practices and daily mindfulness. Designed with a user-friendly interface, Headspace caters to a diverse audience, making it an excellent choice for both beginners exploring the world of mindfulness and seasoned practitioners looking to deepen their practice.

   One of the standout features of Headspace is its **themed meditation series**, which address specific needs such as stress reduction, improved sleep, and heightened focus. For golfers, the focus series is particularly valuable, guiding users through meditations that sharpen concentration and mitigate anxiety—both critical for performing under pressure on the course.

   In addition to these targeted meditation sessions, Headspace offers **quick workouts** that provide concise, effective mindfulness exercises for those with busy schedules. These short, impactful sessions allow golfers to integrate mindfulness practices into their day, whether it's a pre-round boost to set a positive tone or a calming exercise between rounds.

   Headspace also features a variety of **sleep aids and soundscapes** designed to enhance relaxation and promote restorative sleep. This is especially advantageous for athletes, including golfers, who often contend with the mental stresses associated with competition. By utilising these calming soundscapes and guided sleep meditations, users can ensure they receive the recovery essential for optimal performance on the course.

   Overall, Headspace serves as a comprehensive resource that supports golfers in cultivating mindfulness, enhancing their ability to navigate challenges with clarity and focus while also fostering an inner sense of peace. By harnessing the app's features, golfers are empowered to not only improve their mental game but also enrich their enjoyment of the sport through a more mindful approach to practice and play.

2. **Calm:** Calm is a highly acclaimed mindfulness app recognised for its exquisite design and extensive library of resources, including guided meditations, soothing sleep stories, and relaxing music. Its primary goal is to improve mental health by fostering mindfulness and promoting relaxation, making it an essential tool for those seeking to enhance their overall well-being.

   One of the standout features of Calm is its collection of **meditations tailored to address various issues** such as anxiety, self-esteem, and focus. For golfers, the focus meditations are particularly relevant, as they guide users in developing concentration and mental clarity—key components for executing shots under pressure. These tailored sessions provide golfers with targeted techniques to calm their minds, allowing them to approach each round with a sense of purpose and unwavering focus.

   In addition to meditation sessions, Calm offers a unique selection of **sleep stories narrated by well-known voices**. These captivating narratives not only aid listeners in achieving restful sleep but also provide a gentle way to unwind after a demanding day of play. For athletes, restorative sleep is critical for recovery and performance; therefore, these soothing stories can significantly contribute to a golfer's overall well-being.

   Another notable aspect of Calm is its library of **music and nature sounds**, which can be used to accompany meditation or serve as a calming backdrop throughout daily activities. The thoughtfully curated soundscapes, inspired by nature, create an immersive experience that enhances relaxation and mindfulness. Golfers can leverage these calming sounds while practicing, using them to create an ambiance that promotes concentration and peace.

   Overall, Calm stands out as a comprehensive resource that not only supports mindfulness practices but also enhances the overall experience of golfers both on and off the course. By utilising Calm's features, golfers can cultivate a serene mind-set, reinforce their mental game, and ultimately enrich their enjoyment of the sport. Embracing this app into your routine empowers you to navigate the challenges of golf with clarity and confidence while providing the necessary tools to foster mental resilience and well-being.

3. **Insight Timer:** Insight Timer distinguishes itself as a premier mindfulness app renowned for its extensive library of free guided meditations and insightful talks from experienced teachers and

mindfulness experts. With thousands of resources available, it caters to a wide array of interests and needs, making it an invaluable companion for those seeking to deepen their mindfulness practice and enhance their overall well-being.

One of the standout features of Insight Timer is its **vast selection of resources**, offering a diverse range of meditation types that cater to various aspects of personal growth and mental health. Golfers can explore meditations focused on improving concentration, managing anxiety, and building confidence—all of which are essential skills when stepping onto the course. The breadth of topics available means that users can tailor their meditation experience to meet specific needs, whether they are preparing for a round or seeking to cultivate a greater sense of calm and clarity in their daily lives.

Additionally, Insight Timer boasts **community features that allow users to connect and share experiences**. This social aspect is particularly beneficial for golfers, as it fosters a sense of belonging and support among like-minded individuals. Engaging with a community of practitioners not only enhances motivation but also provides opportunities for shared learning and encouragement, turning solitary practice into a communal journey.

The app also offers **regular events and workshops on mindfulness topics**, featuring expert-led sessions that span a variety of interests. These events can help golfers deepen their understanding of mindfulness and incorporate new techniques into their routines. Participating in workshops allows golfers to engage with the broader mindfulness community, gaining insights that may enhance both their game and personal well-being.

Furthermore, Insight Timer includes a built-in **timer for self-guided sessions**, allowing users to create their own meditation routines. This feature is particularly relevant for golfers who wish to integrate mindfulness seamlessly into their practice, whether it's a dedicated session focusing on breath awareness or a short visualisation practice before a round. The flexibility of self-guided meditation can empower golfers to cultivate a deep sense of presence tailored to their individual needs.

In summary, Insight Timer is more than just a meditation app; it is a comprehensive resource for those seeking to cultivate mindfulness in their lives. By utilising its extensive library, engaging with the community, and participating in events, golfers can enhance their mental game significantly. Embracing Insight Timer as part of your mindfulness toolkit can lead to not only improved performance on the course but also a greater sense of fulfilment and connection in all areas of life.

4. **Breathe:** Breathe is an innovative app designed specifically to assist users in managing stress and anxiety through the power of breath work and mindfulness. With its intuitive and user-friendly interface, Breathe makes it effortless for golfers and individuals alike to incorporate mindful breathing into their daily routines, fostering a greater sense of calm and focus.

   One of the app's key features is its **tailored breathing exercises**, which cater to various situations and personal goals. Whether you're preparing for a challenging round, feeling overwhelmed by the pressures of competition, or simply seeking a moment of tranquillity in your day-to-day life, Breathe offers exercises that can be customised to meet your needs. These guided sessions can help you manage anxiety effectively, allowing you to re-centre your thoughts and emotions quickly.

   Additionally, Breathe provides **guided meditations** focused on relaxation and stress reduction, making it an ideal companion for golfers both before and after their rounds. These meditation sessions are crafted to help users release tension, clear their minds, and cultivate a state of calmness—essential for maintaining focus and composure during play. Golfers can use these meditations not only to prepare mentally for competition but also to unwind and recover after a strenuous round.

   Another valuable feature of the Breathe app is its **progress tracking** capability. This function allows users to monitor their mindfulness journey over time, providing insights into their breathing practices and overall well-being. By tracking your progress, you can identify patterns and improvements, encouraging you to stay committed to your practice. This aspect is particularly beneficial for golfers, as it cultivates a sense of accountability and reinforces the importance of making mindfulness a regular part of their training.

   In summary, Breathe serves as an essential resource for golfers looking to enhance their mental game and manage stress effectively. By utilising the app's tailored breathing exercises, guided meditations, and progress tracking, you equip yourself with powerful tools to foster mindfulness both on the course and throughout your daily life.

Incorporating Breathe into your routine not only helps you stay calm and focused during competitions but also enriches your overall experience and enjoyment of the game, allowing for deeper connections to both golf and yourself.

5. **Smiling Mind**: Smiling Mind is a thoughtfully designed mindfulness app developed by psychologists and educators, aiming to provide tailored mindfulness programs for various age groups and settings, including schools and workplaces. The app stands out for its commitment to making mindfulness accessible and relevant to users of all ages, making it an excellent resource for golfers looking to enhance their mental game while fostering emotional resilience.

One of the key features of Smiling Mind is its **age-appropriate mindfulness programs**. Whether you're a junior golfer just starting on your journey or a seasoned player seeking to refine your mental skills, the app offers programs specifically designed to meet diverse developmental needs. This ensures that each user can engage with mindfulness practices that resonate with their unique experiences, maximising the benefits of the training.

Each session within Smiling Mind is **developmentally focused**, thoughtfully crafted to cultivate emotional regulation and resilience. By incorporating techniques that encourage self-awareness and coping strategies, golfers learn to manage their emotions more effectively both on and off the course. This is particularly relevant for navigating the emotional highs and lows that can accompany competitive play, empowering athletes to maintain composure and clarity amid pressure.

Additionally, Smiling Mind features **progress tracking**, allowing users to monitor their engagement with mindfulness practices over time. This feature not only helps reinforce a commitment to a regular mindfulness routine but also enables golfers to see measurable improvements in their mental strength and emotional well-being. Understanding your journey can be motivating, inspiring you to continue incorporating mindfulness into your training.

Furthermore, the app provides **relaxation techniques** suitable for users of all ages, making it a versatile tool for golfers seeking quick methods to reduce stress and anxieties associated with competition. These techniques can be woven into pre-round rituals or used during breaks, promoting a sense of calm in high-pressure environments.

In summary, Smiling Mind serves as a vital resource for golfers who want to integrate mindfulness practices into their routines. With its tailored programs, focus on emotional regulation, progress tracking, and accessible relaxation techniques, the app empowers athletes to cultivate a resilient mind-set and enhance their overall performance. By engaging with Smiling Mind, golfers can transform their mental game, allowing them to approach each round with confidence and a deeper connection to the sport they love.

Recommended Books on Mindfulness

Books on mindfulness offer a treasure trove of insights into the theories, techniques, and practices that can elevate your understanding and application of mindfulness in daily life, particularly within the context of golf. These texts not only provide foundational knowledge but also share practical strategies that can be seamlessly integrated into your golfing routine. Here are a few essential reads that stand out for their relevance to mindfulness in the sport:

1. **"The Miracle of Mindfulness"** by Thich Nhat Hanh
In this classic work, renowned Zen master Thich Nhat Hanh elucidates the essence of mindfulness and offers practical exercises to cultivate a mindful mind-set. His teachings on being present in each moment resonate deeply for golfers, reminding players to appreciate the simplicity of each shot and the beauty of the course, ultimately fostering a more joyful experience of the game.

1. **"Wherever You Go, There You Are"** by Jon Kabat-Zinn

    This book is a comprehensive introduction to mindfulness meditation and its applications in every aspect of life. Kabat-Zinn emphasises how living mindfully can transform the way we engage with our experiences. For golfers, this message is crucial; it encourages players to be present, reducing performance anxiety and enhancing focus on the course.

2. **"The Mindful Athlete"** by George Mumford

    George Mumford draws on his experiences working with elite athletes to illustrate how mindfulness can be employed as a tool for peak performance. His guidance on cultivating mental strength and emotional resilience is particularly beneficial for golfers who face high-pressure situations, providing them with practical techniques to perform under stress while maintaining composure.

3. **Radical Acceptance"** by Tara Brach

   This illuminating book explores the concept of accepting oneself fully, flaws and all. Tara Brach offers readers tools to embody self-compassion and embrace challenges, which is vital for golfers who experience anxiety or frustration during competitive play. Learning to accept both successes and failures without harsh criticism can lead to a more enjoyable golfing experience.

4. **"Mindfulness for Beginners"** by Jon Kabat-Zinn

   Offering a practical approach to starting a mindfulness practice, this book guides readers through foundational techniques that can be beneficial for both daily life and sports. For golfers, the lessons in this book provide a solid grounding in mindfulness that enhances focus, emotional clarity, and overall enjoyment on the course.

By immersing yourself in these essential reads, you can deepen your understanding of mindfulness and equip yourself with the tools needed to enhance your performance both in golf and in daily life. Their insights will help you cultivate a more resilient and positive mind-set, allowing you to navigate the complexities of competition with grace and composure. These books ultimately serve as valuable resources in your journey towards integrating mindfulness into your golfing practice and enriching your overall experience of the game.

Online Courses and Websites

In addition to apps and books, a wealth of online courses and websites provide structured programs dedicated to the practice of mindfulness. These resources offer valuable tools for golfers looking to deepen their understanding and application of mindfulness techniques, ultimately enhancing their performance and overall experience in the sport.

1. **Mindful.org:** Mindful.org serves as a comprehensive hub for information related to mindfulness practice, offering a diverse range of articles, resources, and online courses. This platform covers various aspects of mindfulness and meditation, making it an invaluable resource for golfers seeking to understand the principles that can enhance their mental game. By exploring the content available on Mindful.org, players can gain insights into effective mindfulness strategies, learn how to integrate these practices into their routines, and deepen their connection to the sport.

2. **The MBSR Online Course by the Centre for Mindfulness in Medicine, Health Care, and Society:** The Mindfulness-Based Stress Reduction (MBSR) online course, led by trained instructors, spans six weeks and focuses on cultivating well-being through mindfulness practices. This structured program is particularly beneficial for golfers, as it teaches participants techniques to manage stress, increase focus, and foster emotional resilience—essential qualities for optimal performance on the course. Engaging in the MBSR curriculum equips players with practical tools that can be directly applied during competition, enhancing their mental clarity and composure.

3. **Coursera Mindfulness Courses:** Coursera features a wide array of mindfulness courses taught by experts from accredited universities and institutions. These courses cover various aspects of mindfulness, including meditation techniques, mindful leadership, and applications in daily life. For golfers, the insights gained from these courses can be directly translated into enhanced concentration, emotional regulation, and resilience on the course. By enrolling in these programs, golfers can learn evidence-based techniques and strategies that refine their mental game, allowing them to perform at their best in high-pressure situations.

4. **The Greater Good Science Centre:** The Greater Good Science Centre offers research-based information on mindfulness, compassion, and emotional well-being. This resource is particularly valuable for golfers seeking to enhance their mental state and foster a deeper understanding of mindfulness's role in their lives. The website features a wealth of articles, guided meditations, and practical tools that support the cultivation of mindfulness in everyday life. By utilising these resources, golfers can integrate mindful practices not only when playing but also in everyday interactions, enhancing their overall connection to themselves and others.

5. **10% Happier:** Founded by journalist Dan Harris, 10% Happier is a platform that includes both a podcast and an app centred around mindfulness and meditation. The site features insights from mindfulness experts and offers guided meditations tailored for busy lifestyles. For golfers, the practical, accessible content provided by 10% Happier serves as an excellent introduction to mindfulness techniques, allowing players to effortlessly incorporate mindfulness into their daily routines. The combination of expert guidance and practical tools makes this resource a valuable companion on the journey to enhanced focus and emotional balance in both life and sport.

Community and Retreats

For those seeking to deepen their mindfulness practice, engaging with mindfulness communities or participating in retreats can offer invaluable support and insights. These communal experiences allow golfers to connect with others who share similar passions, facilitating personal growth and enhancing their understanding of the practice. Below, we explore how each avenue can enrich your mindfulness journey, particularly in the context of golf.

1. **Local Mindfulness Groups:** Many cities host local mindfulness groups or meditation centres that provide regular classes and community events. Joining such groups creates rich opportunities for connection with others who are equally invested in cultivating mindfulness. This environment not only fosters a sense of belonging but also allows you to share experiences and learn from experienced instructors.

   For golfers, local mindfulness groups can be particularly beneficial as they often offer workshops tailored to specific themes, including stress management and performance improvement. Interacting with fellow athletes can provide insights into different approaches to mindfulness and how these techniques can be applied to enhance your game. The camaraderie built within these groups reinforces accountability and encourages continual growth.

2. **Mindfulness Retreats:** Attending a mindfulness retreat can be a transformative experience, immersing participants in an intensive mindfulness practice over an extended period. These retreats typically focus on silent meditation, yoga, and mindful living, offering a perfect opportunity to disconnect from the daily distractions of life and deepen your practice.

   For golfers, retreats can significantly enhance mental resilience and focus, as they allow for uninterrupted time dedicated to cultivating mindfulness. The serene environments often found at these retreats create a conducive atmosphere for self-reflection, helping individuals reconnect with their intentions and aspirations in both golf and life. After experiencing a retreat, many golfers report feeling rejuvenated, more centred, and equipped with practical techniques they can integrate into their daily routines and competitive play.

3. **Online Mindfulness Communities:** In our increasingly digital age, numerous online platforms and social media groups foster communities focused on mindfulness practice. Engaging with like-minded individuals in these virtual spaces can provide encouragement, motivation, and shared experiences that enhance your understanding and application of mindfulness.

   Online mindfulness communities are especially beneficial for golfers who may not have access to local groups. These platforms offer a wealth of resources, including guided meditations, forums for discussion, and opportunities to participate in virtual events or challenges. Connecting with fellow golfers in these settings allows you to broaden your perspective on mindfulness techniques and gain insights into how others effectively apply these practices in their games.

Conclusion

Embracing the various online courses and resources outlined throughout this book offers golfers a significant opportunity to enhance their mindfulness practice, ultimately leading to improved performance and a more enriching experience on the course. These platforms present structured learning, expert insights, and practical tools tailored specifically to the needs of athletes, empowering you to cultivate greater awareness, emotional resilience, and enjoyment of the game. The integration of these valuable resources will not only transform your golf performance but will also profoundly influence your overall approach to life.

Engaging with community-based resources and retreats further deepens your mindfulness practice while enhancing your well-being. Whether through local mindfulness groups, immersive retreats, or vibrant online communities, these experiences provide essential support, motivation, and shared learning opportunities. For golfers, participating in these avenues amplifies individual practice and fosters a rich sense of connection to both the sport and fellow athletes, thereby enriching the overall golfing experience and promoting holistic growth.

As you navigate the world of mindfulness, remember that an array of resources stands ready to support your endeavours. Mindfulness apps, insightful books, online courses, and community engagement serve as valuable tools to deepen your understanding and practical application of mindfulness in daily life. Incorporating these resources into your routine can significantly enhance your experience on the golf course while positively influencing your quality of life.

It is important to recognise that mindfulness is a continuous journey of exploration. Remaining open to learning and adapting along the way is key to maximising the benefits of your practice. By embracing the challenges and joys that accompany mindfulness, you cultivate a resilient, focused, and balanced existence that impacts not only your golf game but all facets of your life.

As you seek out the resources that resonate with your personal journey, know that each step taken toward cultivating mindfulness is an investment in your overall well-being. Whether you dedicate a few minutes to meditation via an app or immerse yourself in an engaging book that sparks your curiosity, these experiences will shape your path toward a more mindful and enriching life. Embrace the transformative power of mindfulness, and watch as it enhances your performance on the golf course and nourishes your journey in the game of golf and beyond.

8.2: Interviews and Stories from Golfers Who Practice Mindfulness

In the competitive world of golf, mindfulness has emerged as a cornerstone for enhancing performance and supporting personal well-being. By integrating mindfulness practices into their daily routines, numerous golfers have undergone profound transformations that extend far beyond the greens. The journey of mindfulness is not just about improving one's game; it encompasses a holistic approach to managing mental challenges, emotional resilience, and overall quality of life.

In this chapter, we share compelling interviews and inspiring stories from golfers who have wholeheartedly embraced mindfulness as part of their training and personal development. Through their narratives, these athletes illuminate the substantial impact that mindfulness practices have had on their games, mental states, and overall experiences with the sport they love.

The golfers featured in this chapter offer unique insights into how mindfulness has influenced their approach to both practice and competition. You will hear first hand accounts of how specific techniques—such as mindful breathing, visualisation, and loving-kindness meditation—have helped them navigate the pressures of the game with greater poise and clarity.

Additionally, these stories reveal how mindfulness has enriched their everyday lives, fostering stronger relationships, enhancing emotional well-being, and instilling a greater appreciation for their experiences on the course. By showcasing the journey of these golfers, this chapter serves as both inspiration and a practical guide for anyone seeking to enhance their own performance through mindfulness.

As we delve into these personal narratives, allow yourself to be inspired by the profound transformations that mindfulness can bring. Through their experiences, you will discover that the practice is not just a tool for success in golf; it is a pathway to greater joy, connection, and fulfilment, making every swing and every round a cherished part of their journey in the sport.

Interview with Professional Golfer Sarah Thompson

Background: Sarah Thompson, a professional golfer ranked among the top 20 players in the Ladies Professional Golf Association (LPGA), is widely recognised for her calm demeanour, particularly during high-pressure situations. Her ability to maintain composure on the course has made her a formidable competitor and an inspiration to many aspiring athletes.

Q: How did you first get introduced to mindfulness, and why did you decide to incorporate it into your practice?

Sarah: My journey into mindfulness began during a sports psychology seminar, where I first heard about the concept. The idea of being fully present and focused resonated deeply with me. I had always struggled with nerves during tournaments; my mind often felt cluttered with distractions that hindered my performance. I realised that in order to improve my game and enjoy the overall experience of playing golf, I needed to explore mindfulness as a practice.

Q: Can you describe how mindfulness has influenced your game?

Sarah: Practicing mindfulness completely transformed my approach to golf. I have developed a mindful pre-shot routine that helps centre me every time I prepare for a shot. I take a few deep breaths, visualise my swing, and focus on the moment—allowing no outside distractions to interfere. This mindful focus has been instrumental in lowering my stress levels and boosting my performance. I find that I'm no longer overthinking or second-guessing myself; instead, I am engaged in the task at hand.

Q: *What specific mindfulness techniques do you use during competitions?*

Sarah: I rely heavily on breathing techniques, especially in tense moments, such as during critical putts. I consciously practice slow, deep breaths to calm my nerves, which helps me stay present in the moment. Visualisation also plays a key role in my preparation before each round. I visualise the specific shots I will take and how I want the ball to travel, keeping my mind focused on execution instead of worrying about the potential outcomes.

Q: *How has mindfulness impacted your life outside of golf?*

Sarah: Beyond golf, mindfulness has significantly affected my relationships and day-to-day activities. I've developed a gratitude practice where I reflect on three things I'm thankful for each day. This practice helps me to appreciate the little moments in life, extending beyond just my successes on the course. Overall, I notice that I feel less anxiety, which contributes to a more balanced and healthier mind-set.

Source: Thompson, Sarah. Insights shared in interviews featured in Golf Digest and various sports psychology articles.

Story of Amateur Golfer Mark Rodriguez

Background: Mark Rodriguez is an amateur golfer who embarked on his journey into competitive golf just two years ago, participating in local tournaments. Initially, his enthusiasm for the sport was overshadowed by the anxiety he experienced during competitions, prompting him to seek a better approach to improve his mental game.

Mark's journey into mindfulness began after a particularly stressful tournament, in which he performed poorly despite feeling well-prepared. The frustration he felt in the aftermath of that experience sparked a desire for change in how he approached golfing. Determined to overcome his anxiety, he discovered a mindfulness workshop hosted by a local golf club. Intrigued by the potential benefits, he decided to sign up, eager to learn techniques that could help him manage his stress and enhance his performance.

During the workshop, Mark learned valuable techniques such as breathing exercises, meditation, and positive self-talk, all of which inspired him to incorporate mindfulness into his regular routine. "I remember my first tournament after starting my mindfulness practice," Mark recalls. "I developed a solid pre-shot routine where I would take deep breaths and visualise the shot before hitting the ball. Instead of fixating on my score or worrying about what others were thinking, I concentrated solely on the swing itself."

The results of integrating mindfulness into his game were palpable and transformative. Mark found himself playing with renewed confidence and significantly less anxiety. He came to appreciate the process involved in executing each shot, no longer feeling overwhelmed by the pressure of competition. "Practicing mindfulness taught me that every shot is an opportunity to learn," Mark explains. "I started to view mistakes as stepping stones rather than failures. This shift in mind-set helped me relax and, ultimately, improved my performance."

After several months dedicated to mindfulness practice, Mark re-entered the local tournament circuit with a fresh perspective. This time, he placed in the top ten across multiple events, marking a significant achievement in his golfing journey. More importantly, Mark experienced a profound shift in his self-perception; he played more confidently and truly enjoyed his time on the course.

"Mindfulness changed how I approach golf and life," Mark concludes. "I've learned that it's not just about the outcome; it's about being present for the ride." His story serves as an inspiring reminder of the powerful influence mindfulness can have, transforming challenges into opportunities for growth and reinforcing the joy inherent in the game of golf.

Source: Rodriguez, Mark. Insights shared in interviews and articles featured in local sports publications and golf community forums.

Interview with Veteran Golfer Tom Branson

Background: Tom Branson is a seasoned golfer with decades of experience under his belt. Throughout his extensive golfing career, he has made mindfulness a foundational component of his game, particularly as he transitioned into senior competitions. His insights into the mental aspects of golf offer valuable perspectives on how mindfulness can enhance performance and overall enjoyment.

Q: *How do you incorporate mindfulness into your practice, especially after years of playing?*

Tom: After many years in the game, I recognised that I had developed some less-than-ideal habits, particularly in high-pressure situations. This realisation prompted me to explore mindfulness and weave it into my routine. It's all about being aware of my thoughts and feelings without judgment, allowing me to approach the game with a clearer mind-set and more intention.

Q: *What are some key techniques you emphasise in your training?*

Tom: A major focus of mine is on breathing techniques and visualisation. Whenever I'm on the course, I take a moment to ground myself with my breath before each shot—it has become a ritual for me. I inhale deeply, hold my breath for a moment, and then exhale slowly. That simple act calms my mind and allows me to return to the present, helping maintain a sense of focus. I also visualise each shot, picturing the trajectory of the ball and how I want it to land. This aspect of my practice has become crucial, especially as I strive for consistency in my game.

Q: *How has mindfulness impacted your experience on the course, particularly in stressful situations?*

Tom: Mindfulness has fundamentally transformed how I experience pressure while playing. In the past, I often let anxiety take control. My nerves would overwhelm me, leading to mistakes that I knew better than to make. Now, when I feel that pressure building, I remind myself to concentrate on my breath and the intentions I've set for each shot. This practice allows me to acknowledge the pressure without being overwhelmed by it, which is genuinely liberating!

Q: *What advice would you give to younger or less experienced golfers looking to incorporate mindfulness into their games?*

Tom: Start simple—there's no need to overhaul your entire routine overnight. Just carve out small moments throughout your round to check in with yourself. Take a breath, observe your surroundings, and appreciate the game as it unfolds. Celebrate your victories, no matter how small they may be. And when you make mistakes, acknowledge them without harsh judgment. Instead, use these moments as opportunities to learn and grow. Remember, each round is part of your journey as a golfer, contributing to your overall development and enjoyment of the sport.

Source: Branson, Tom. "Mindfulness in Golf: Personal Insights from a Veteran Player." Insights shared through interviews featured in golf publications and podcasts

Story of Junior Golfer Lisa Chen

Background: Lisa Chen is a dedicated junior golfer who embarked on a mindfulness journey to manage her anxiety levels during competitions. At just 16 years old, she found herself grappling with performance anxiety that often surfaced during tournament play. The pressures from school, her golf team, and self-imposed expectations weighed heavily on her young shoulders, leading to missed opportunities and disappointing results on the course.

After a candid conversation with her coach, Lisa was introduced to mindfulness practices specifically aimed at helping her manage stress and anxiety. Inspired by the potential benefits, she committed to daily meditation and began employing visualisation techniques to enhance her performance.

"I remember the first tournament I played after starting my mindfulness practice," Lisa shares. *"Before teeing off, I took some time to breathe deeply and visualise my shots, imagining a smooth swing and the perfect contact with the ball."* This intentional approach allowed her to settle her nerves and embrace the moment with confidence.

The results of her newfound mindfulness practice were nothing short of remarkable. Rather than being consumed by anxiety, Lisa felt empowered and purposeful during her rounds. *"Mindfulness changed how I feel on the course. Instead of focusing on what could go wrong, I learned to concentrate on what I could control—my swing, my mind-set, and my enjoyment of the game,"* Lisa reflects, highlighting the transformative impact that mindfulness has had on her performance.

As she continued to adopt this mindful approach, Lisa cultivated a joy for the game that had previously been overshadowed by the immense pressure of competition. *"Now, I approach every tournament as an opportunity to learn and grow. I still feel nervous, but it doesn't control my performance anymore. I embrace it,"* she explains, a smile illuminating her face.

Lisa's story serves as an inspiring testament to the power of mindfulness in overcoming challenges. By actively engaging with mindfulness techniques, she has not only improved her performance on the golf course but also rekindled her passion for the game. Her journey underscores the notion that mindfulness can empower athletes of all ages to navigate the intricacies of competition with grace and resilience.

Source: Chen, Lisa. "Finding My Game: How Mindfulness Helped Me Overcome Anxiety." Interviews featured in youth sports publications and golf community forums.

Conclusion

The stories and insights shared by golfers like Sarah, Mark, Tom, and Lisa illustrate the profound and transformative role mindfulness can play in enhancing performance, fostering resilience, and enriching the entire golfing experience. Through their journeys, they have demonstrated that by thoughtfully integrating mindfulness into their routines, individuals can cultivate a deeper connection to the game and significantly alter their experiences on the course.

Mindfulness empowers golfers to navigate the complexities of their performance with clarity and purpose. It encourages players to prioritise self-compassion, allowing them to treat mistakes as opportunities for growth while celebrating successes with gratitude. In this context, mindfulness serves as a vital tool that not only supports individual development but also nurtures overall well-being, reinforcing a positive relationship with the sport.

The common and lasting improvements that mindfulness has proven to achieve—from increased focus and reduced anxiety to enhanced enjoyment and emotional regulation—underscore its value in the world of golf. The ability to remain present in the moment fosters greater mental clarity, enabling golfers to execute shots with confidence and purpose while enjoying the journey of improvement.

As you contemplate incorporating mindfulness into your own golfing journey, draw inspiration from the experiences of these athletes. Explore various techniques and experiment with practices that resonate with your personal style and needs. Discover the mindfulness strategies that not only enhance your performance but also deepen your enjoyment of the sport.

Remember, each golfer's journey is unique—embrace yours with an open heart and a mindful spirit. By committing to the practice of mindfulness, you unlock the potential to not only excel in your game but also experience a more fulfilling and enriched connection to golf. Ultimately, this journey transcends the game itself, guiding you toward greater presence, resilience, and joy in all aspects of your life. Embrace mindfulness, and watch as it transforms your golfing experience into one of growth, connection, and lasting fulfilment.

Printed in Great Britain
by Amazon

dad35888-7172-4f54-9b47-12ec868b1661R01